MEDICAL
AESTHETICS
SUCCESS

REGISTER YOUR BOOK NOW AND RECEIVE SPECIAL GIFTS

- A revenue potential Capacity Calculator to realize your business's true cpabilities.
- A complimentary Success Planning session.
- A $500 gift card toward any seminar.

These gifts will provide you a jumpstart to a successful path!

THERE ARE TWO WAYS TO CLAIM YOUR GIFTS:

1. Go to InSPArationManagement.com/gifts
2. Scan this QR code

Need help? Email us: Info@InSPArationManagement.com

MEDICAL AESTHETICS SUCCESS

YOUR BUSINESS IN THE BLACK

DORI SOUKUP

Copyright © 2022 by Dori Soukup, Orlando, Florida

All Rights Reserved

No part of this publication may be reproduced, stored in a retrieval system, or transmitted in any form or by any means electronic, mechanical, photocopying, recording, scanning or otherwise, or translation of any part of the work beyond that permitted in Section 107 or 108 of the 1976 United States Copyright Act, without prior written permission of the copyright owner. Requests for permission or further information should be addressed to InSPAration Management, LLC.

This publication is designed to provide accurate and practical information in regard to the subject matter presented. It is sold with the understanding that the publisher is not engaged in rendering legal or accounting services.

Published by InSPAration Management, LLC

131 Executive Circle

Daytona Beach, FL 32114

InSPArationManagement.com

Printed in the United States of America

Praise for Dori Soukup

We love all the strategies InSPAration Management and Dori provide the medical aesthetics industry! I have known Dori for several years, and whether you are a veteran or just getting started, I recommend that you tap into all the great business tools she provides to help you succeed.

— *Shelby Miller DNP, Ruma Aesthetics, Utah*

As a founder of Rêvée Aesthetics, I love all the guidance and tools we receive from Dori and her team. They are a group of professionals who are skilled business experts in the medical aesthetic field. They've helped us grow exponentially and expand our business to a bigger location.

— *Dr. Lonny Green, Rêvée Aesthetics, Virginia*

Before you go into business, or attempt to improve it, you need an effective business model to follow and implement. We own a plastic surgery center and two Medspa locations. Our locations are thriving, causing us to expand again. We love being members of InSPAration Management and highly recommend and thank them for their guidance and support in our success. If success is your destination, they will help you get there.

— *Lynda & Dr. T. Lazaro, Aestique Medi Spa and Aestique Plastic Surgery, Pennsylvania*

As a physician and founder of Renew Medspa and Renew Training Institute, I believe that education is always a key to success. Whether it's clinical, such as what we offer or what InSPAration Management offers, continued education is a must. No need to reinvent the wheel—there are available solutions to follow and successful models you can implement. Don't delay your success with trial and error. Soar ahead by applying the principles that Dori writes about. They work!

— *Dr. Lisa Vuich, Renew Medspa and Renew MediSpa Training Institute, New Hampshire*

As a business owner for over 30 years, I thought I knew it all until I met Dori and discovered her business model. With two locations and over 100 employees, I decided to join her program, and I'm very glad I did! Now fast forward a few years, my business runs on autopilot due to all the systems and structures Dori and her team helped us implement. We are now more profitable than ever!

— *Denise Dubois, Complexions Day Spa, Salon & MedSpa, Albany and Saratoga Springs, New York*

I am very grateful for all the gems I have learned today. For someday beginning in this journey, I feel like I am not drifting in the sea anymore. I have a clear path to my MILLIONS now.

— *Dr. Arlene Rillo, Amalurra Centre for Medical Aesthetics, Las Vegas, Nevada*

Introduction

Thousands of medical aesthetic professionals, industry leaders, and teams have learned the business principles and strategies in this book which I developed and perfected over the past 20 years. They are now enjoying a higher level of success due to their implementation efforts.

My success as a global speaker, author, seven-figure business advisor, and CEO of InSPAration Management, along with my clients' success, led me to write this book so the entire industry can benefit.

The enclosed medical aesthetics business strategies are designed to help you take your business from **red to black**, or from **average to super successful**.

My goal is to provide you with a proven-effective, easy-to-implement business model so you can accomplish your mission and exceed your goals. Get ready to replace stress, frustration, and slim profit lines with peace, harmony, love, joy, exponential growth, profit, and success!

After all, life is too short to reinvent the wheel. We all have better things to do with our lives than endless trial and error. We were put on this planet for a purpose, and mine is to make your life easier and help you succeed in business the fastest way possible.

This is my fourth book, and it's probably not my last because I'm passionate about my life's purpose, and I love writing and sharing my voice with professionals like you. I'm also very blessed to be surrounded by a great family, friends, colleagues, team, and clients and to be doing what I love most. Developing business models that work and sharing them with people like you is what brings joy into my life, and success to you!

My life didn't start out this way. As the youngest of five children, I was always playing "catch up" with my brothers and sisters. And as we got older, that didn't change. I always felt I had to keep up with them, especially because they are all super successful entrepreneurs.

I was the only one in my family who chose to work in the corporate world, where I spent 18 years in the hospitality industry. My career started in an entry-level position at a resort in Orlando, Florida, and I climbed the corporate ladder to vice president. What most impacted my success was continual education, personal development, studying, practicing, learning new things, reading, and surrounding myself with positive individuals and great mentors. That's what helped me advance my career quickly and succeed.

As a young executive in my early 20s, I knew I needed to expand my knowledge, I attended every business seminar that came to Orlando. I bought and read tons of business books and listened to many cassettes (it was a while ago, lol). I studied them over and over. From Tony Robbins to Brian Tracy and Zig Ziglar, you name it, I read or listened to them or attended their seminars. I had a burning desire for education and success, I was a sponge.

That passion and desire to succeed led me down a path to become a trainer and a developer of business educational programs. Through education and training, I was able to help my team and oversee one of the most productive resorts within the chain.

When I'd reached the highest level and my head was hitting the glass ceiling, I decided to start my own consulting firm and become an entrepreneur. I left a very profitable corporate position and started on my own with nothing except my knowledge, passion, and drive.

You may be in the same situation. Maybe you're an MD who's tired of the conveyer belt of patients or an Urgent are Physician, NP, PA, or RN who works in a hospital and wants to go into the medical aesthetics field. Or maybe you're a corporate person like I was and now you want to open a medical aesthetics practice.

Or maybe you're already in business and are looking for ways to grow and become more successful.

No matter where you are now, decide to go all in. I think people with one foot in and one foot out fail. You need to burn the ship and not look back. That's what I did. It wasn't easy, but it was doable.

Being an entrepreneur takes a lot of courage, drive, commitment, passion, and faith. It's not easy to give up a secure position to venture into the unknown.

When I left my VP position, my husband Craig was a stay-at-home dad, and my son Charlie (now 25) was three years old. We were accustomed to a very nice lifestyle, and everyone thought I was crazy for leaving my job. But that was the problem—it was only a job. I wanted more.

So I took a leap of faith and started my business. I rented a small executive suite and started working hard and smart.

Today, I have a beautiful office building in Daytona Beach, Florida, that's more than 7,000 square feet, with a full video production studio, I have a great team, and we're growing exponentially.

We focus on helping people like you generate millions of dollars in their medical aesthetics business. We offer business seminars, webinars, consulting, coaching, and marketing strategies that include the 4 S's: proven effective systems, structure, strategies, and solutions.

I didn't just wake up one morning or wave a magic wand and voila, it happened. Getting started took a lot of dedication, long hours, and motivation.

My business consulting started with day and resort spas. Then, when the medical aesthetic business started becoming more popular, we shifted to accommodate that need for industry growth. I traveled all over the world, to more than 40 countries, learning more about everyone's businesses and discovering their challenges.

When I got home, I came up with business solutions to help business owners overcome those challenges. The business solutions we offer are all tested and proven effective, and they are a result of more than 20 years of research and development.

The InSPAration Management business model is the most complete and proven-effective medical aesthetic business-specific model I'm aware of in the industry. The model is available on MedSpa Biz University, a site where all members can access all aspects of the business model for easy implementation and success!

My passion is to help others reach a higher level of success. As a business advisor and mastermind leader, I've had the pleasure of changing people's lives for the better. Every day I'm so thankful I have that opportunity to contribute, and I thank God for all my blessings. The fact that you are reading this book is a blessing for both you and me.

This is ideal for any professional who works in or owns a medical aesthetic practice, spa, or wellness center or anyone considering venturing into the beauty & wellness industry.

This book contains four parts and 12 chapters.

Part One - Mindset and Success

Mindset is where everything begins. You will discover the proper foundation needed to succeed with everything you

- **Chapter One** describes the 10 principles needed to become a high achiever
- **Chapter Two** helps you identify your current habits and how to implement new habits to live a successful and happy life.
- **Chapter Three** will guide you on how to welcome change, adapt, and innovate to continually grow personally and professionally.

Part Two - Marketing and Positioning Strategies - Become your Consumer's Best Choice!

- **Chapter Four** will help you improve your positioning to reach a higher level of success. When consumers find you, you only have a few seconds to impress them and entice them to reach out. In this chapter, you will discover key factors you can implement to improve your positioning and become the go-to person in your community for medical aesthetics, wellness, beauty, health, etc.
- **Chapter Five** - Gain celebrity status to compete and gain market share. Today, competition is fierce, more than ever before. To succeed you must differentiate, gain celebrity status, be noticed, and be recognized for your expertise. You will read how you can achieve this status with video marketing.
- **Chapter Six** – Increase your capacity with economical marketing strategies. In this chapter, you will discover super economical and easy-to-implement marketing

strategies to help you increase traffic to your medical spa and revenue.

- **Chapter Seven** – Elevating your Success with Reviews and Testimonials Today's consumers check reviews and testimonials before they make their choices. What others say about you matters and could lead to success or failure.

  You can build your business by tapping into this underutilized marketing strategy by your team. Discover easy ways to ask for and gain testimonials, and reviews and watch more consumers contact your medical practice, and increase traffic.

Part Three - Improving your Guest/Patient Experience and Your Retention Rate

- **Chapter Eight** – Discover a new super successful business model

  In this chapter, you will discover how to generate a lead and take them through a journey that will result in them being a lifetime client. You will be introduced to a super successful business model that will help you move away from an a-la-carte model – meaning one client visit and done, into a customized program and then into a VIP member and a lifetime client.

- **Chapter Nine** – Enhancing your guest experience with touchpoints

  If you want to increase your client's retention rate, then it's time to improve your guest experience with touchpoints. In this chapter, you will discover adjustments you can make to your guest experience so your guests would say "WOW this was the best experience ever". Touchpoints can be implemented within all aspects of the medical aesthetics guest experience leading to higher client satisfaction, increased retention rate, and elevated success!

Part Four - Reaching Success Without Being Salesy

- **Chapter Ten** – Financial health – your medical aesthetics business in the black

  The subtitle of this book is "Your Business in the Black". Every chapter was written to help you improve your business and take you in the black.

  The heart of your business is the sales process. You can have the most beautiful facility with the greatest medical lasers and medspa treatment menu but if you don't have a proven effective sales process, you will be in the red. In this chapter, you will discover essential sales to help you and your team become more successful.

- **Chapter Eleven** - Tapping Into Online Revenue Streams

  Today, you have great opportunities to include multiple revenue streams within your business, yet many medspa owners miss out on this opportunity. In this chapter, you will learn how to increase your revenue by implementing a wide range of online revenue streams.

- **Chapter Twelve** - Succeeding with a recurring revenue model and a loyalty program

  The information in this chapter will totally change your business and financial health.

  Having a recurring revenue model will give you cash flow security, reduce your marketing cost, and increase retention. Imagine generating six figures per month from only your recurring revenue model. That's what InSPAration Management members accomplish, and you can do the same.

We're fortunate to be in an industry that's growing exponentially. The medical aesthetics business is here to stay, thanks to all consumers who care about their appearance and wellness and are willing to invest top dollars into looking their best.

As you enter this field, my responsibility is to lead you down the right—successful—path. My team and I take this very seriously, and we're always striving to provide you with the best business solutions available.

Thank you for purchasing this book, remember to register your book and claim the gifts provided. We wish you great success.

Go to InSPArationManagement.com/gifts

HOW TO GAIN THE MOST FROM READING THIS BOOK

Everyone learns in different ways. I recommend that you first read this book all the way through. As you read, highlight, underline, and write down your takeaways at the end of each chapter. Repetition is key to learning, I encourage you to read through the book a few times.

You may even discover that you're already familiar with some of these principles. If so, ask yourself if they are currently part of your business model. It's one thing to be familiar with a principle, but it's another to have it as part of your business model.

You'll also see *Shortcuts to Success* sections at the end of each chapter. These tips are designed to help you realize your next steps and get started on the right path.

Also, I've included some InSPAration Management business tools to help you succeed in the fastest way possible. I make these recommendations not to sell to you, but to help you.

This book's subtitle is *Your Business in the Black*. Black is what you want in business. When your company is in the black, it's profitable, financially secure, and not overburdened by debt. I want you to have a debt-free business that's thriving and generating multiple millions of dollars annually. We have helped many clients get into the black, and we want to help you, too.

Imagine your business on auto-pilot, debt-free, and extremely profitable! That's what you can expect when you implement the business principles outlined in this book.

Begin living the life you want!

DEDICATIONS

I dedicate this book to my mentors, colleagues, clients, family, and friends. Thank you for all your support, guidance, and encouragement!

A special dedication to Craig Soukup, my best friend and the father of my son. I miss him tremendously and wish him a happy eternal life!

To my son Charlie, for being strong, loving, and for pursuing higher education in environmental science. He wants to make a difference in the world. Your dad would be very proud.

CONTENT

Introduction 7

Part One Mindset and Success 21

Chapter 1. Ten Principles to Becoming a High Achiever 23

Chapter 2. Implement and Live Successful Habits 45

Chapter 3. Welcome Change, Adapt, and Innovate 59

Part Two Positioning and Marketing Strategies 69

Chapter 4. Improve Your Expert Positioning 71

Chapter 5. Gain Celebrity Status and Differentiate Your Business with Video Marketing 83

Chapter 6. Increase Revenue with Economical Marketing Strategies 97

Chapter 7. Elevate Your Success with Reviews and Testimonials 119

Part Three The Guest Experience and Retention 135

Chapter 8. Five Steps to a Successful Lifetime Client Journey 137

Chapter 9. Touchpoints to Enhance the Guest Experience and Increase Retention 155

Part Four Success Without Being Salesy 169

Chapter 10. Financial Health –Your Business in the Black 171

Chapter 11. Tap into Online Revenue Streams 189

Chapter 12. Succeed with a Recurring Revenue Model and Loyalty Program 207

Part One
Mindset and Success

CHAPTER 1

TEN PRINCIPLES TO BECOMING A HIGH ACHIEVER

> *Whatever the mind can conceive and believe, it can achieve.*
> —Napoleon Hill, Think and Grow Rich

What comes to mind when you think of high achievers? Consider super athletes like Michael Jordan and Tom Brady, celebrities such as Oprah Winfrey, artists like Rihanna, or influencers like Gandhi, Martin Luther King, and Mother Teresa. We all know of many high achievers who've changed the world for the better.

Maybe you are a high achiever already, if so, congratulations! I would encourage you to still read this chapter and be open to the ten principles discussed because we can always improve.

In this chapter, we'll guide you through setting a solid foundation so you, too, can become a high achiever and reach the peak level of success.

The first and most important factor in becoming a high achiever is "you." You have to decide to become one. You're reading this book, you may already be one. But we can always do even better.

Thoughts and actions lead to being average, good, or a high achiever. They determine whether we succeed or fail. The actions and choices you make either provide you with a rich, happy, and fulfilled life or keep you at a level where your work is average and unfulfilled.

Now is the time to decide and commit to becoming a high achiever and do whatever it takes keep improving!

> *The quality of a person's life is in direct proportion to their commitment to excellence, regardless of their chosen field of endeavor.*
> —Vince Lombardi

Once you're committed to becoming a high achiever, the question becomes: "What do I need to know and do to become a high achiever and have a successful life?" The answers are in this book.

I discovered the answers while working in the medical aesthetics industry over the past 20 years. I continue to have the pleasure of acting as a multiple seven-figure business advisor to many medical professionals, entrepreneurs, and team members.

Those experiences allow me to identify patterns in behaviors, characteristics, and actions that determine who is most likely to succeed and who will fail.

Unfortunately, we see failing patterns every day when business owners first reach out to us and tell us what's not working in their business. Many businesses lack structure, systems, cash flow and most operate under a Wild-Wild West business model.

The good news is that it's usually fixable.

My goal is to provide you with a successful path. I'm offering you the best practices, effective principles, easy-to-implement habits and patterns, and all the skills you need to become a high achiever.

Napoleon Hill's "Whatever the mind can conceive and believe, it can achieve," from his best-selling book *Think and Grow Rich*, is a great quote. A friend recommended this book to me when I was 19 years old and had just started my career in the hospitality industry. I owe some of my professional and personal growth and success to applying the principles from that book. *Think and Grow Rich* gave me the foundation I needed, which led to who I am today. It helped me design a super successful life.

We can often put failing patterns into one or more of three main categories. We call this "lack of GMA," for short.

Patterns of failure	Patterns of success
G - No **goals**, no plan	Setting clear goals with a strategic plan
M - The wrong **mindset**	Always positive and expecting the best
A - No **action**; procrastination	An action plan with implementation strategies

Replace these medical aesthetic business patterns of failure with the patterns of high achievers.

GOALS

A lack of defined goals, quotas, targets, plans, measurements, rewards, and consequences are failing patterns. Most businesses, we discovered, don't have well-defined financial goals or a plan on how to achieve and measure them. Many put no attention on monitoring performance and numbers. When a company has no defined financial goals, its team also has no goals. The entire company simply goes through the motion of showing up to work every day without a definite purpose or goal in mind.

"No goals, no action plan" means average results, and that's no place to be. Set clearly defined goals and when you achieve them you are a high achiever.

MINDSET

Having the wrong mindset regarding the sale process, selling, or making recommendations—thinking it's a bad thing—is a huge failing pattern. Many providers are afraid to make recommendations because they don't want to be seen as a salesperson. They don't recommend enough high-ticket programs, nor do they recommend home care products. That's actually the worst failing pattern because their guests do not receive the treatments they need to look their best. It also limits the provider's income and causes the business to be in the red instead of the black. This mindset causes businesses and teams to be average.

Change the mindset, and you change the outcome. Study mindset, and you'll be able to design a great life.

ACTION

The wrong action, or a lack of action and implementation, is the kiss of death. Everyone has good intentions, but if you take the wrong or no action, then nothing changes, and nothing improves. Often we see no implementation of an effective business model, no training, no systems, no strategies, and no solutions to make the business and team improve performance. Operating and working in a medical spa with no strategic plan, clear actions, or implementation plans, lead to average returns or even a decline in performance.

These are just three of the most common failing patterns we see, correct, and replace with principles of great success. There are many more, and I'll share some of them with you in upcoming chapters. I'll provide solutions to overcome failing patterns on how you can avoid them and become a high achiever.

A note on "average." Some people think average is okay, and it is—if you want to be like everyone else.

Many statistics indicate industry averages. Let's begin by defining the average, so you can aim higher.

- The average medical spa generates $1.2 million in gross revenue, yet only nets between 5% and 15% in profit.
- The best medical spas—the high achievers—generate $5 million in gross revenue and net 20% or more in profit.

Make a choice now. Say goodbye to average and become a high achiever instead. You can chart a path toward becoming the best of the best, a high achiever, by applying these 10 principles of success.

10 PRINCIPLES TO BECOME A HIGH ACHIEVER

Apply the following 10 principles into action and establish a solid foundation for your success.

1. **Determine your big dreams**

Whether you're an entrepreneur, leader, manager, team member, or work as a provider or a guest relations professional, you owe it to yourself to dream and dream big. Everything begins with a dream, a thought.

Buy a *New Dream Journal* and write down all your big dreams.

- Everything you want to accomplish
- The things you want to own
- The type of house you want to live in
- The car you want to drive
- Vacations you want to take
- The schools you want your children to attend
- The charities you'd like to support
- The positive impact you want to make
- The type of life you want to live

No matter where you are now in life, start dreaming big. Believe that anything is possible. You must believe and have faith. Write down what you really want and picture it in your mind's eye.

Live each day with purpose, working toward accomplishing your dreams. Leave average behind and dream big! Know that abundance is all around you. Dream it. Live as though you've already achieved your dreams.

2. **Find your purpose**

Purpose needs to be the central motivating factor in your life.

When you get up in the morning, get yourself ready, go out, do what's right and fulfill your purpose in helping others.

Make sure you're on the right career path. If you've chosen a career strictly because of how much money you can earn, you might not be aligned with your purpose. You might be in the wrong career, field, or industry. It can't be only about money.

Identify your purpose, and then make sure it's meaningful and comes effortlessly. Your desire must truly be focused on helping your clients with the transformation they want while you build lasting relationships with them.

> *If you help enough people get what they want, you automatically get what you want.*
> —Zig Ziglar

Purpose guides you through your goals and decision-making processes. It offers direction to your life and gives it meaning.

Start to find your purpose by answering some questions.

- Why did you choose a career in the medical aesthetics or spa industry?
- Why did you accept this position or role?
- What value do you provide your clients?
- What value do you add to the team and business?
- What do you want to accomplish?

- How do you make a difference?
- What positive impact do you make?
- Who do you serve? How do they benefit?
- How can you become an expert in what you do?
- What career path would you like to take going forward?

I encourage you to carefully define your purpose. Commit to meaningful work and live with purpose. That will help you become a high achiever.

3. **Have a burning desire**

Notice I say "burning" desire—not just a desire. There's a big difference between the two.

Burning desire is one of the principles I learned from *Think and Grow Rich*. A burning desire fuels your goals. There are many stories about how burning desires can fuel your dreams and set them on fire. Here's one of my favorites:

The actor Jim Carey started out as a big dreamer with a burning desire to become famous. He wanted to achieve great things by becoming a movie star, but like many new actors, he struggled. One day early in his career, he went to the top of the Hollywood sign and sat there overlooking Hollywood and Los Angeles. He imagined himself as a big movie star, making movies and earning millions of dollars.

One night, he wrote himself a check for $10 million and put it in his wallet. He told himself, "One day, someone will pay me $10 million to act in a movie." Sure enough, when he got his role in the movie *The Mask,* he was paid $10 million. The rest is history.

You can achieve anything you set your mind to, but first, you need to dream it and then back up that dream with a burning desire to achieve it. Dream it, believe it, take action, and have faith that it's possible to achieve your goals.

You can tap into endless opportunities and create your own successful path. Everything and anything is possible when you dream it and go beyond just desire. Nurture your burning desire and achieve.

Dream it, believe it, achieve it!

4. **Mindset, and maximizing your potential**

People often put limits on themselves with thoughts of self-doubt and fear. Their mindset and self-talk are negative instead of positive. They tell themselves, "I'm not good at this or that," "It's just my luck," or "I can't raise my prices because everyone will leave."

Their mindset is focused on what they can't do instead of what they can. It's not focused on their unlimited potential. Mindset can help you succeed, or it can help you struggle and fail.

A large skincare company once reached out to my firm to consult and help them increase sales. During the assessment phase, I asked the team, "How much do you think a Medical Spa owner should invest in an opening order to fill their boutique and start out in the retail business?"

They said, "We currently ask for a $1,000 opening order." Frankly, I was in shock at that answer. I was thinking, "That's how much one customer should be purchasing." Obviously, they had the wrong mindset.

The fact is, that "When you expect a little, you receive a little." That's the wrong mindset. It's limited thinking. It's a thought process that can limit you from having a great lifestyle and the ability to increase your income.

During training, I asked the team to start requiring opening orders to be at least $5,000 and guess what happened. Yes—they began selling $5,000 orders.

Nothing changed except the team's mindset. The team expanded its thinking. It tapped into a higher potential. That's how a strong mindset is. One simple shift allowed the company and team to experience exponential growth and greatly expand their potential.

That example can apply to many companies and positions within the medical aesthetic industry. Many people have the wrong mindset and have limiting beliefs about what they can and cannot achieve and receive.

AN INJECTOR'S MINDSET SHIFT TO SUCCESS

Another example is an injector who worked for a client and friend of mine. She hired a nurse practitioner (NP) to do medical aesthetics at her medspa. The injector was simply doing Botox and a little filler here and there, and she averaged about $350 per client.

My friend knew they could help their consumers more and do much better financially. They became InSPAration Management members and reserved a Strategic Day with me. She and her NP came to my office, and we worked on their business model, mindset, systems, strategies, and goals.

We realized her NP needed to recognize the extent of her professional obligation. She needed to shift her mindset from a la carte guest experiences to creating Customized Personal Improvement programs for her clients. (This is part of the S.A.C.R.E.D. system, which we discuss in Chapter 12.) She learned this and began practicing and applying it.

Within two weeks, she was offering her clients customized transformations. Using Customized Programs, she was truly helping them, and she began generating between $4,000 and $10,000 per consultation.

It was a simple system, strategy, and mindset shift that quickly started creating triple-win outcomes:

1. The clients are happy and seeing better results.
2. My friend is happy and generating more profits.
3. The NP is happy, qualifying for big bonuses and earning high achiever's rates.

Shift to a growth mindset, tap into unlimited potential, become a high achiever and maximize your worth!

5. **Set ginormous goals**

A Harvard Business study found a direct correlation between goal setting and success. It said that **14 percent of people with goals are 10 times more successful than those without goals**.

Grant Cardone writes about goal setting in his book *The 10X Rule*. He says, *"The only difference between success and failure is that most people set the wrong goals—often too low."*

You've been told to set achievable goals. But set ginormous ones instead. That way, even if you don't achieve them, you still achieve way more than you would have by setting lower, more achievable goals.

Do you think Olympians say, "I don't want to break a world record," or "I don't need a gold medal; I just hope I finish the race?" I don't think so. But that's what most people do. They just go through the motions of being average.

There's nothing worse than being average in a dead-end career.

Let's say you're an aesthetician. Are you going to be an aesthetician for the rest of your life? If that's what makes you happy—if it's your purpose—fine.

But maybe you have a burning desire to advance and become a master aesthetician, the best aesthetician ever, to achieve your true worth and fulfill your purpose. That's a great goal.

Or maybe you want to advance and become a department lead. You might want to become a spa or medspa supervisor or work your way up to director. Maybe you want to be a practice manager or own multiple locations. The opportunities are endless.

Growth in the medspa and spa industry is exponential. It's your turn to tap into your true potential and seize the opportunities to keep improving and moving up.

Write your goals in your journal and start reading them every day. The more detailed your goals are, the faster you can become a high achiever.

6. **Choose your inner circle**

> *Who you spend time with, is who you become! Change your life by consciously choosing to surround yourself with people with higher standards!*
> —Tony Robbins

Your inner circle consists of people who are close to you and who understand you. It's the people you trust to always be there when you need them.

Who's in your inner circle?

Think about who you spend time with and how they affect your life. Do they help you find peace of mind and harmony in your life? Do they encourage you and fill your life with positivity?

Or do they create chaos in your mind with their doubt and negativity, or their ideas of limits on what you can and cannot do?

You decide who stays and who should leave your inner circle.

If your friends and colleagues are negative, always complaining, never satisfied, always nagging, and hardly ever smile, those aren't the people you should associate with. Those people are not high achievers. You don't want to be around them or like them.

Your inner circle must be filled with people who are positive and supportive. In addition to your inner circle, it's wise to have a great mentor, coach, or business advisor who has your best interest at heart.

Check your associations, surround yourself with the right people, and become a positive force yourself. Be the person everyone wants to be around because you're happy, joyful, energetic, peaceful, and helpful. Be an expert and a leader.

Remember the industry we're in. Consumers come to you to be replenished with happiness and to feel and look better. If you're not that way yourself, how will you help your clients achieve their goals? How will you fulfill your own purpose?

Remove the negative people from your life. I know it's difficult, but it must be done. If they are raining on your parade they will cause negativity and keep you from achieving your goals.

Make it a rule to keep improving your inner circle. Fill it with great people who will help you, while you help them become better. Improve each other's lives so all of you can achieve what you want.

7. Invest in personal development and expertise

One of the biggest challenges I hear from owners, founders, and CEOs is that their teams are not very engaged. They lack motivation and do just enough to keep their job.

The InSPAration Management membership benefits include access to the *MedSpa Biz University* platform. That's an online, private-member university where business training for each position is available on demand.

When owners and leaders ask their teams to attend this training, the first thing out of their team members' mouths is often, "Am I going to get paid for training?" Owners are investing in their teams, yet they get this pushback on attending. They are attempting to help the team grow professionally, yet some members resist.

The last thing anyone should ever ask an owner—who's already paying for the training programs—is whether they will be paid to attend. When someone is paying for your training, your self-improvement, you should respond, "Okay, what time do you want me there?" Asking if you're going to be paid for training is the behavior and mindset of someone happy to be average.

When someone wants to invest in you by inviting you to attend training meetings, go. Attend with bells on. Say, "I'm so excited!" Thank them for the opportunity to become a better professional and a high achiever. Becoming an expert requires not only being driven and passionate, but also investing time and money in personal development.

Your training must include a clinical and business curriculum, which we discuss in a future chapter.

Train like you're going to the Olympics, where someone is always breaking a record. (How does that happen?) It proves that all of us can do better.

Look at your own performance and see how you can improve it. Invest in your education, personal development, and becoming an expert, master, and high achiever.

Every day, invest time in your personal development. Read, listen, watch training videos, role play, own the process, and achieve results. Shift your mindset, set huge goals, dream big, and reach your true potential.

Deep down, you *know* you can do a lot better than you're doing right now. We all can.

8. **Drive and determination**

Drive and determination are two characteristics that separate winners from losers. You must have both if you want to succeed in life—even when you don't feel like it.

Quarterback and team leader Tom Brady won seven Super Bowls! How did he do it? By using his drive and determination. By having a burning desire to become the best of the best. By sharpening his skills, practicing, studying, and being a leader with his teammates. He fulfilled his role as the captain of the team.

The New England Patriots gave up on Tom after he helped them win six Super Bowls. He took his drive and determination to a new team, the Tampa Bay Buccaneers, and won his seventh Super Bowl in his forties. Incredible!

Tom Brady's story demonstrates many of the principles discussed here. If he can do that, why can't others? They can, but most don't practice the principles. They don't have a burning desire, drive, and determination.

In sports, they don't just give the team a football and say, "Show up to the game and throw the ball around." They have a coaching team, game plan, strategies, structure, discipline, and more.

They have different positions for offense and defense. Every person in every position knows their role and the contributions they make. When each team member has a defined role and knows exactly what's expected of them, everyone is more likely to be a high performer who contributes to the big goal.

What's your role in the company? Are you driven and determined to accomplish your goals? Are you accountable for your efforts, performance requirements, skills, knowledge, and expertise?

Measure your progress and always be training. Train, train, and train some more. Remember that being driven and determined are key principles to becoming the best of the best.

9. **Maximize your value and income potential**

> *Most folks are about as happy as they make up their minds to be.*
> —Abraham Lincoln

I've trained thousands of leaders and their team members in the past two decades. When I ask, "Do you know how to maximize your income potential?" the answer is usually, "I have an idea how much I can make per year."

When I ask providers, "Do you know how much more income you could be generating from retail sales?" I often hear, "No."

The list goes on. Most don't know their true income potential, worth, or how to maximize their value.

That's a failing pattern. A high achiever knows his or her numbers. A high achiever realizes that's a key principle to succeeding.

How to reverse-engineer income goals for providers.

- Decide how much income you want to earn in one year.
- Calculate different scenarios for how you could earn that amount of money.

If you're part of the InSPAration Management community, you're probably familiar with the compensation model we teach and offer, *The Volume Per Guest Complan – A Performance-Based Compensation Model.*

The VPG compensation model includes the following pay mix:

- Hourly or base salary
- Bonuses based on revenue generated
- Benefits
- Rewards for Key Performance Indicators

Based on your current pay model, calculate your true income potential based on you being the best of the best. Gather your reports and calculate the following:

- How many hours do you work per month?
- How many clients do you see per month?
- What is the average revenue per client for both treatment and retail?
- What is your total revenue?
- What are your contributions to the business? What values do you bring?
- How much revenue do you help the business generate?

- How much are you earning? Calculate an income case scenario:
- If you want to make $X, you need to see at least X clients per month.
- Each client must spend $X amount per visit.
- Each client must purchase $X amount in retail.
- If you're a provider and you hit all the bonuses and targets, your income would increase by $X.

When an employee contributes to the business's success in a big way, the business owner generally realizes this and rewards the employee accordingly. But if the employee is not contributing as a high achiever, the owner can't pay employees a top dollar guarantee, for just appearing at work.

It's essential to know your potential income at the highest level of productivity. Find the answers. Set high income goals.

If you're a business owner who wants to maximize productivity, revenue, and profits, I recommend you watch the *Leap Ahead* on-demand business and leadership seminar. It presents an A to Z blueprint on operating a profitable and thriving business.

There are endless opportunities to increase your income, and this book is designed to help you reach your ultimate income goals.

10. **Design your success with imagination**

> *Whatever you imagine, big or small, will be reflected in the world around you.*
> —Neville Goddard

The last of the 10 principles is probably the most important one.

Many philosophers and scholars have taught about the power of imagination, yet few people focus on the transformations and joy it brings.

Neville Goddard firmly believed that imagination creates reality. Read what he said again: "Whatever you imagine, big or small, will be reflected in the world around you."

He lectured extensively on the importance of imagination and allowing your mind to wander to where your desire is while letting go of the current reality.

Napoleon Hill also talked about imagination. He wrote, "The *imagination* is the workshop of the soul, where are shaped all the plans for individual achievement."

He said, "If you do not see great riches in your imagination, you will never see them in your bank account."

And he wrote, "Man's only limitation, within reason, lies in his development and use of his imagination."

> **Imagination is more important than knowledge.**
> —Albert Einstein

Design your success first in your imagination. See how you want it to be, and it will come true.

You may be thinking, "Wow, Dori, now you're really out there," but this is true. I've seen it work both in my own life and in that of my inner circle.

When you visualize your success in your imagination, you start noticing what you need to do to make it a reality. Then what you want starts to appear.

Neville described imagination as thinking from the end, meaning what you want to manifest. Feel it, smell it, taste it, and hear it—and then feel the sense of accomplishment that you achieved it.

Imagination has no limits. It's yours and yours alone, and it allows you to experience a completely different world inside your mind. It lets you look at every option and mentally design your own successful future. It can help you be more creative and more innovative.

It can help you do and be anything you want to be, simply by imagining it. You want to be a high achiever? Imagine what that would feel like. What will you be doing? Where are you living? Who's around you? What do you do with your free time?

Let your imagination run wild. See yourself as a high achiever, having already achieved that status. Go ahead and explore the power of your imagination with no limits, no restrictions, and no reality. Simply imagine and design your success.

> *Without imagination, innovation dies. Keep imagination alive and succeed!*
> —Dori Soukup

I encourage you to think deeply about these 10 principles, make a plan, and begin implementing them in your life.

Begin by assessing your current philosophy and mindset. Then create a list of improvements you'd like to achieve and start taking action to become a high achiever.

TAKEAWAYS

_____

_____

_____

_____

_____

_____

_____

SHORTCUTS TO SUCCESS

- Buy a journal and begin imagining your bright future.
- Design your success using your vivid imagination.
- Do the "dream big" exercise.
- Define your purpose.
- Know and set your income goal.
- Determine your inner circle.
- Discover the education and skills needed to elevate your expertise in your field.
- Practice the 10 principles to becoming a high achiever.

INSPARATION MANAGEMENT BUSINESS TOOLS

- The Leap Ahead Leadership Seminar, available live and on-demand
- The VPG Compensation model – a performance-based pay plan

CHAPTER 2

IMPLEMENT AND LIVE SUCCESSFUL HABITS

> *Quality is not an act, it is a habit.*
> —Aristotle

> *Motivation is what gets you started. Habit is what keeps you going.*
> —Jim Rohn

To become a high achiever, you'll need to develop successful habits. In this chapter, we define good habits and discuss how they shape a successful future.

It's important to understand that habits are acquired behaviors. Behaviors become habits when you repeat them for several days in a row. Repeating an action is what forms a habit.

For example, you probably have the same morning and evening routines. That's because you have repeated your actions many times, and that routine is embedded in your unconscious mind.

You may have heard that it takes 21 days to form a habit. But there's also the 21/90 theory, which was born in 1960 when cosmetic surgeon Dr. Maxwell Maltz wrote the self-help book *Psycho Cybernetics, A New Way to Get More Living Out of Life*.

A study conducted at University College in London found that it takes people at least 66 days before a habit feels so automatic and natural it becomes part of a lifestyle.

Some studies indicate that 90 percent of normal behavior is based on habits. It's important to make sure those habits are good ones that will help you achieve great things.

We develop habits whether we realize it or not. For example, I notice that people attending our multiple-day business seminars and events, such as the *Leap Ahead*, the *Millionaires' Circle*, or the *Become Published* seminar, choose a seat on the first day and then sit in the same seat each day afterward. Why? Because humans are habitual.

A successful future is determined by your daily routines and habits.

We're going to define habits and share eight successful habits. You can learn and apply these habits to improve and accelerate your progress to becoming a high achiever, reaching and exceeding your professional and personal goals.

HABIT CATEGORIES

Habits are formed by repeated actions and usually fit into one of two categories: personal or professional.

1. Your **personal habits** may be spiritual or involve family, friends, leisure time, or something else. They might include golfing, traveling, socializing with friends, reading, or shopping. What do you usually do on your days off?

2. Most of your habits are probably **professional habits** because you're at work more than anywhere else. What are your work habits? What do you do when you first get to work? What are your client relations and guest experience protocol habits? How do you respond to your clients' habits? How do you communicate with leadership and team habits? What are your educational and personal development habits?

In your journal, write down your habits and categorize them as personal or professional.

I recommend two books to help you understand habits better: *The Power of Habit* by Charles Duhigg, and *The 7 Habits of Highly Effective People* by Stephen Covey. Some of the information in this chapter are strategies I learned from these books.

THE HABIT LOOP

Charles Duhigg writes in-depth about how habits are formed. He calls it the "habit loop" and discusses how to change bad habits into good habits.

His three stages of a habit loop are:

The cue. That's the trigger, a stimulus, which tells the brain to go into automatic mode and choose a habit to perform.

The routine. The habit itself, which can be physical, mental, or emotional.

The reward. This helps the brain determine if this specific habit loop is worth remembering for the future. If the brain finds the reward beneficial, it will try to perform the action again in the future. That's how a habit develops.

Duhigg talks about Pepsodent toothpaste as an example of habit. In the early 1900s, toothbrushing wasn't the norm.

Claude Hopkins wanted people to have healthy teeth, so he created Pepsodent toothpaste, which left your mouth with a tingly feeling.

The cue was feeling filth over your teeth and wanting to clean them. The routine was to brush your teeth with Pepsodent. The reward was your mouth having a tingling feeling and your teeth feeling clean.

Even though the tingling has nothing to do with clean teeth, the reward was enough to hook the world on toothpaste. People's brains wanted the tingling feeling, so they formed the habit of brushing their teeth.

Stephen Covey described habits differently. He saw them as intersections of knowledge, skill, and desire. Knowledge is what you want to do and why, skill is the way you do it, and desire is the motivation.

IDENTIFYING GOOD AND BAD HABITS

After you write down and categorize your habits, identify each one as good or bad. Dig deep and be honest with yourself.

Good habits lead to increased productivity, a healthier lifestyle, and becoming a high achiever.

Bad habits don't. Identify your bad habits and form plans to improve or replace them.

Managers often complain about employees who are frequently late, don't meet their goals, and fail to communicate well. These employees' professional and personal habits drag the business down.

Employees' bad habits may include not being clear about goals. They may be disorganized and not clean their treatment rooms. Some don't recommend retail products. They procrastinate. They're negative and lazy. They're not good with follow-through.

If you recognize some of these bad habits in yourself or your team, it's time to make some changes. Bad habits will kill your career and make it impossible to reach your goals. It's time to convert your bad habits into good ones.

Don't try to change all of your bad habits simultaneously, though. Change them one at a time, starting with the most impactful one. When you replace your bad habits with good habits, you become more productive even without consciously trying. Here's an example. Say you want to create the habit of using the *Don't Sell, Recommend! With the P.R.I.D.E. System* (explained in Chapter 10) to increase sales.

To successfully create the new habit, you must repeat the entire system with every client for several days in a row. Without that consistent repetition, it won't become a habit, you risk forgetting parts of the system in the future, and you won't be as effective.

Remember the "cue, routine, reward" method from *The Power of Habit* when you're implementing the P.R.I.D.E. System.

Cue. The guest has a problem. They want to look younger/rejuvenate/hydrate, etc.

Routine. It should be automatic for you to recommend a solution from among your treatments and products.

Reward. The client is happy and sees better results. You fulfilled your purpose, boosted your self-confidence, and felt great self-satisfaction for helping them. You also increased your income. Everyone wins!

> *Excellence is an art won by training and habituation. We do not act rightly because we have virtue or excellence, but we rather have those because we have acted rightly. We are what we repeatedly do. Excellence, then, is not an act but a habit.*
> —Aristotle

8 HIGH-ACHIEVER HABITS FOR SUCCESS

Excellence is a habit. That's so well said! The following will help you prevent bad habits from developing. It will help you create and implement successful habits that lead to a more fulfilled and purposeful life.

1. Think with the end in mind

Always think with the end in mind. This is my favorite habit from Stephen Covey because it forces me to think about the outcome before starting a project or even doing something as simple as going to the grocery store.

For example, when I go into the office, I already know what I need to accomplish. I know my priorities and who I am helping that day. I know what outcome I want.

Thinking that way makes you much more productive and means a higher rate of guest satisfaction and retention.

That's why I recommend and teach the importance of conducting **Daily Success Planning (DSP)** meetings.

Make the DSP meeting a habit. Meet every morning and see how you can help people that day. What end results do you want? Do you want to discover your opportunities, foresee what to recommend to each client, and decide how you can help them more with treatment upgrades?

Identify new clients on your schedule and determine your day's actions. The DSP meeting is about planning your daily success while thinking about the outcome and ending each day on a high note.

Practice this habit of thinking with the end in mind in everything you do, and you'll be much more successful in both your professional and personal life.

I practice this habit daily, even when looking for a parking space. I always think a parking spot is waiting for me as I pull into a lot. Sure enough, someone will be pulling out so I can pull in. It's the same with seats in a restaurant and green traffic lights. I picture the outcome I want, and it's there.

Always picture the outcome—the end you want—before starting, and you, too, will accomplish what you want.

2. Positive communication

There are many great communicators, but one of my favorites is Martin Luther King, Jr. and his "I Have a Dream" speech. Another is Oprah Winfrey, who built an empire using her excellent communication skills. Good communicators connect with their audiences on an emotional level.

> *People will forget what you said and did, but they will never forget how you made them feel.*
> —*Maya Angelou*

Positive communication takes place when you "*seek first to understand, then to be understood*," according to Stephen Covey. Sometimes people are too quick to judge, or they give a bad answer. They don't take the time to listen and understand what someone is saying.

We have two ears and one mouth, which is a good reminder to listen twice as much as we talk. Don't be in such a rush to judge. Hear your clients' desires and needs. Know what your children want. Remember that these habits can be applied throughout your whole life, not just your professional one.

Be positive and understanding. Compliment people. Be open to differences. Be kind. Doing this will let you experience positive communication. Making positive communication a habit will also position you as an influencer—someone people want to listen to and hear what you have to say.

3. Be solution-focused

> *You will get all you want in life if you help enough other people get what they want.*
> —Zig Ziglar

Where there's a problem, there's usually a solution. Take the initiative to find the solution to a problem whenever possible. If one of my team members comes to me and says, "We have a problem with this," I reply, "Okay. What do you recommend? What's the solution?" Everyone should be capable of finding solutions to problems.

Be a problem solver. Offer solutions and focus on how you can make things better. The more you train yourself to be solution-focused, the better off you will be because the more credibility and respect you'll gain.

Focus less on the problem and brainstorm for solutions instead. There's always a way to make lemonade out of lemons. Being solution-driven is a great habit to develop and practice.

4. Be productive instead of busy

> **Without a sense of urgency, desire loses its value.**
> —Jim Rohn

Many people's productivity levels change throughout the day. Some are more productive in the mornings, and some at night. Figure out when you are most productive and work during that time.

Pay attention to how you spend your time, and decide if you are completing tasks efficiently. There's a big difference between being productive and just being busy. It's possible to be busy but unproductive. When you're productive, you accomplish more in less time.

There are so many distractions now, such as texting, checking email, social media browsing, and the phone. Some people waste time on unproductive tasks such as scrolling through Instagram, Facebook, and other social media platform for hours. That's not a good habit.

The minutes are precious. Use every one of them to be more productive and get closer to your goals. If you catch yourself doing busywork, stop, regroup, and then call on your good habits to help.

5. Continuous learning and improvements

> *An investment in knowledge pays the best interest.*
> —Benjamin Franklin

Stephen Covey tells a story about a man cutting a tree. He's been working hard for hours but making little progress when someone asks him, "How long have you been at this?"

The first man replies, "A long time."

The other man asks, "Well, why don't you stop and sharpen the saw?"

The first man says, "I'm too busy to stop and do that."

Sharpen the saw. You must stop and sharpen the saw before starting to cut down the tree. Hone your tools, and you don't have to work as hard.

Keep learning and mastering skills. The more you learn, the more you'll earn. It's why I'm so proud of you for reading this book. You're investing time in learning and improving your skills. Always make time for learning and personal growth.

Become addicted to learning, and you will be a high achiever.

6. Think win-win-win

Some business people think they need a "win-lose" scenario to succeed. They may win the battle with that philosophy, but they'll lose the war. It's not a good practice.

Practice "win-win-win" in every transaction—that's a triple win where the client, provider, and business all win. Achieving a triple-win means you're headed for success.

Whether you're performing treatments, doing a consultation, or welcoming someone to your spa, think about how you can make the engagement a great experience for the client. Always think win-win-win. Create solutions and make recommendations that mean everyone wins.

7. Always be professional

The more professional you are, the more likely you will attract the right clientele and build a strong career or a business.

If you're trying to attract affluent people, stepping up your professionalism is a must. Check your image and communication style and commit to delivering five-star experiences such as the Ritz-Carlton, the Four Seasons, and the finest restaurants. Notice how those fine establishments communicate, how well-trained their teams are, and how they treat their clients.

It's easy to shine these days because so many others are average.

A great work ethic is key to being a high achiever. Be reliable, honest, loyal, and credible. Focus on building great relationships with everyone you come into contact with. Make being a professional a habit and watch your career soar.

8. Measure your performance daily

If you don't measure your performance every day, start now. Keep track of how many treatments and retail sales you generate, the referrals you gain, the clients you enroll in the VIP program, and your retention rate. Measure everything you do and determine whether or not you're improving. Get into the habit of measuring everyone's performance daily.

Monitor whether or not you're hitting your targets. You can't correct and improve actions you aren't measuring. When you make measuring your performance a habit, you'll become an expert in your field.

These eight habits work together to promote a healthy life balance. Applying them will help you reach success on autopilot.

I encourage you to implement these habits into your life. They will help you build the foundation you need to become a high achiever.

TAKEAWAYS

_____

_____

_____

_____

_____

_____

_____

SHORTCUTS TO SUCCESS

- Assess your current habits.
- Categorize them.
- Identify good and bad habits.
- Make necessary improvements.
- Plan to implement new good habits.

INSPARATION MANAGEMENT BUSINESS TOOLS

- Reserve a private executive coaching session.

CHAPTER 3

WELCOME CHANGE, ADAPT, AND INNOVATE

> *Change is the law of life. And those who look only to the past or present are certain to miss the future.*
> —John F. Kennedy

We can't discuss a solid foundation without addressing change and how to best manage and benefit from it.

Change isn't something we can fight. It happens to all of us.

As discussed in the previous chapter, we are habitual creatures. Humans like habits and routines. Repetition makes us comfortable. It's why most people have difficulty with change and avoid it whenever they can.

In my company, we have to manage change daily, while helping business owners and teams implement the business model we teach. Often, teams get comfortable with their positions and stick to their routines. The last thing they want to do is adjust to something new and be uncomfortable.

Employees often think, "Why do we need to change? We don't want to change. We want things to stay as they are. Let's keep doing the same thing over and over again."

That's why we teach them a seven-step process to **managing change successfully.**

In a professional situation, one hopes that every change is for the better. You must realize that change is good. Change relates to self-improvement and business improvements, which are essential to achieving better results. Better results require new or different actions. That's why having an open mind and accepting change is crucial to everyone's success.

The late Dr. Wayne Dyer taught about change often. He said from the minute we are born, we start changing. We start with a baby body, we change to a toddler, we change to a pre-teen, to teen, to young adult, to middle age, to older. Just like our bodies, everything else changes too. Nothing is ever still. So, fighting change is not a wise thing to do.

> *If you change the way you look at things, the things you look at change.*
> —Dr. Wayne Dyer

WORKPLACE CHANGES

Here are some of the common changes that employers and employees experience.

1. Policies, procedures, and new business models
2. Company's vision, mission, and values
3. Compensation plans and benefits
4. Requirements for advanced education
5. Leadership and management skills
6. Team culture

7. Competitive advantage

8. Performance expectations

9. Treatments and products

10. New locations

11. New laws

12. Viruses disruption

13. Client expectations

14. Success levels

Everyone is constantly changing. Your level of talent changes. Your skills change. You experience both big and small changes. It's how you think, and it's your process. Your behavior toward the changes is what separates you from the rest.

You must be able to pivot, innovate, and change. The fact is you will encounter changes throughout your entire life, both personally and professionally, and how you handle those changes can make the difference between you failing or succeeding.

Napoleon Hill discusses the importance of thought in his book, *Think and Grow Rich*. He wrote that "thoughts are things." Telling yourself, "I hate change, I don't want to change, I want things to go back to the way they were," only sets you up for failure. Nothing will go back to exactly how it was before. The only thing that never changes is that change always happens.

Your thought process about change matters. You can either fight it or welcome it.

Think about all the positive changes that can happen in your life. When you start focusing on positive changes, they begin to happen. When your mindset is positive about change, you are on the right path. You adapt and make the necessary adjustments to become more successful.

Never dwell on the past. We only have today, which is why it's called the present. If you control your actions for today, it makes a huge difference in your achievements. Apply your energy towards the present moment and toward achievements.

THE COMFORT ZONE IS THE DANGER ZONE

Some people are stuck in their old ways, bad habits, and bad ways of thinking, and they are happy being in that comfort zone.

Think of change as if you're riding a train. The train is constantly in motion, but it changes track from time to time. The train doesn't have to stop to change tracks. Likewise, you can implement changes without halting everything you're doing.

In fact, you change tracks all the time. You have a track for your morning routine, your work, your loved ones, and so on. You're always changing tracks but never stopping.

Instead of staying in a comfort zone, you can shift tracks by getting a promotion. You could become a department lead, manager, or director. You could expand the business, hire new team members, or open a new location. If you take on a new position, you'll need to make changes. Moving up means changing tracks for the better.

Leave the comfort zone to the average. Stepping out of your comfort zone makes you a high achiever.

Workplace change may be uncomfortable at first, but that's a good thing. You learned how to walk and how to ride a bike. It was uncomfortable the first time, and you may have fallen, but you got back up. And later, you were able to take off the training wheels. You learned how to read and write.

Those are all changes you implemented in the past. You learned new things, adapted, and learned, and you can always do that.

Don't let the following bad emotions interfere with your progress.

- **Denial.** When change is a must, some people feel the change is not necessary and go into denial. Explain why it's taking place and how they can benefit from it.
- **Resistance.** There are always one or two people who resist change. Identify who they are and have a one-on-one meeting with them.
- **Acceptance.** Before change can happen, you need buy-in and acceptance from the team. Changes are generally for the better and have a positive influence on those who accept them. Focus on the positives.

> *Remember what got you here, won't get you there. New action is required!*
> —Marshall Goldsmith

WHEN PLANNING CHANGE, KEEP THE FOLLOWING IN MIND

- Identify what needs to be changed and why.
- Who will the change affect, and how?
- What will happen if you don't make the change?
- Outline the steps of launching the change.
- Describe the outcome of the new vision.

- Identify and share, "What's in it for the team?"

Showing the entire team "What's in it for them" provides a great starting point and helps generate support and buy-in.

7 STEPS TO SUCCESSFULLY IMPLEMENTING AND MANAGING CHANGE

1. Be open-minded.
2. Understand why the change is needed.
3. Know what must change and everyone's role in it.
4. Identify the tools and training available to apply the change.
5. Outline the process of implementation.
6. Detail the desired outcome, expectations, and results.
7. Identify the rewards.

You or your employees may resist change and think, "Ugh, here we go again. What do they want me to do now?" But resisting change blemishes the relationships between you and the rest of the team.

If you're a business owner, would you want someone to resist change and not improve, or would you rather see an employee excited to implement change and improve themself and the business? You probably want the latter, of course.

I hear many managers say that their teams resist change. It doesn't make any sense to me. Open your mind to all the positive changes you can make for yourself and your business. Change helps you fulfill your professional obligations and succeed.

Don't resist change because of fear. Avoid negative thoughts, and don't be the person who complains about making changes. Instead of finding faults in the change, realize all the positive outcomes that can come from it.

WELCOME CHANGE

How can you thrive from change? By making a plan, having open communication, and knowing exactly what the goals are. If these things aren't clear at first, clarify your thoughts. Make a plan as to exactly what needs to change, so that everyone can thrive.

If you and your team unite with a positive attitude, work toward the same goal, and don't let negative people get in the way, you will succeed.

> *It is not the strongest or the most intelligent who will survive, but those who can best manage change.*
> —Charles Darwin

There's no reason to fight change. That's just fighting a losing battle. You started changing the minute you were born, and you change every day.

Be open to change and make the most of it.

SELF-CONFIDENCE AND TRAINING

Self-confidence appears when you are well-trained and ready to implement change. Training equals self-confidence.

Realize that you can achieve anything if you practice and persist. *Persistence paralyzes resistance.* Nothing can stop you if you are persistent, continuously learn, and take advantage of practicing and role-playing to develop your skills.

It's always worth the change when you know the change will make everything better. It's always worth it to become a better person, make more money, and help more clients. These changes will help in both your professional and personal life.

MAKE A DIFFERENCE WITH CHANGE

If you want to improve your positioning, grow your business, receive promotions, and earn more, you must take action.

When I was climbing the corporate ladder, I always performed the position I wanted before receiving a new title. I felt a great amount of fulfillment from doing that. You can do the same. Keep learning and keep changing.

As for the team—you can be a high achiever by making recommendations and suggestions, solving problems, and presenting different points of view. Your team leader will notice how engaged and involved you are and will be very impressed with you. If you have a great idea, share it. Be a problem-solver. You will receive recognition and advance your career.

If you don't stand out, and only do the bare minimum, you will not succeed. You'll stay where you are. Strive to be the best so you can elevate your success. You must voice your opinions, get involved, and offer solutions to improve the business. You can make a big difference in your business, which creates more success for everyone.

Don't think, "No one listens to me. No one will take my ideas seriously." Have confidence that your ideas are effective and will benefit everyone.

Your thoughts and actions determine the quality of your life. Be a high achiever. Be someone who isn't afraid of change. You are an adapter and an implementer. Be the best of the best.

How are you going to deal with change from now on? What mindset is needed to improve your business and your professional career? Be flexible, adapt, and implement change.

TAKEAWAYS

_____

_____

_____

_____

_____

_____

SHORTCUTS TO SUCCESS

- Be open to everything great.
- Accept change and go with it instead of fighting it.
- Stay out of your comfort zone.
- Always pivot, adapt, and be flexible.
- Be positive, and welcome change.

INSPARATION MANAGEMENT BUSINESS TOOLS

Team Training - Recipes for Success modules

Part Two
Positioning and Marketing Strategies

CHAPTER 4

IMPROVE YOUR EXPERT POSITIONING

> *If people like you, they will listen to you, but if they trust you, they'll do business with you.*
> — Zig Ziglar

How you position yourself and your business can lead to success or failure. Positioning is the opinion that consumers make in their minds about you and/or your brand. What they think determines whether they choose you or your competition to help them.

It's important to understand the consumer's buying cycle. Today, consumers have an attachment called a mobile phone. In a second, they can look up anything they want. They have many options. There is no shortage of anything in the world. If they want to get Botox, all they need to do is search "Botox near me" on Google, and thousands of places will appear. They'll start comparing you to others. That's where it all starts.

Consumers are more likely to find you online than anywhere else. Your online presence and positioning are key to you being the chosen one!

Google is a magical place. People love to click around, go from site to site, read, look at pictures, check out reviews, make their comparisons, and then decide to call or text for more information.

This is where you need to do everything possible to **hijack consumers' attention with your positioning. You must convince them that you and your team are experts and that you are the only choice.**

The questions are: What are they seeing, and how do they feel about you and your brand? What impression are you making on them?

How do you differentiate yourself, your menu, and your experience from your competitors?

If you're already in business or working in a medical spa, now is the time to assess your online presence and marketing materials. Have you positioned yourself as an expert that grabs their attention? Or are they clicking away?

If you're just starting out, you're lucky because you can establish a great brand and positioning from the beginning. Make sure you reach out to experts in branding and positioning to avoid costly mistakes. You can always ask us, and we can make recommendations.

DIFFERENTIATE YOURSELF

To create a great identity and position you as an expert, assess the following and make sure you're differentiating yourself in all these areas.

- How you tell your story. Why did you choose this career?
- Your professional image and that of your brand and the team.
- Your treatment menu and products.

- The team's expertise and skills.
- Your pricing and added value.
- Before/after pictures and other results.
- Consumer reviews and video testimonials.
- Articles, blogs, newsletters, and books.
- Transformational case studies.
- Overall online presence.
- Marketing materials.
- Messages—are they clear?
- Ask yourself: Do consumers who search online notice your unique positioning?
- Does your content and its descriptions focus on benefits?
- Are you generating leads from your positioning?

Do a survey. Ask your clients to use three adjectives to describe you, your company, products, treatments, and overall image.

If your brand was a person, how would you describe its personality?

- Is it fun, serious, inspiring, old, boring, not engaging, cheap, expensive, or classy?

Focus on relationship positioning. Today, consumers are very demanding and they're looking for great experiences with added value. They are seeking someone they can trust and feel safe with. They want expertise and results.

The first step in relationship marketing is identifying your target market. Who do you help? Clarify your target market, and then use messages and images that the market can relate to.

Tell your story. Your story should start on the home page of your website. You can have a welcome video. Or you could have the first paragraph of your story with a "read more" button that takes visitors to a landing page, where they can read the entire story or watch a video of you telling the story. Tell them why you are doing this. Share your purpose and passion. Discuss why you do this type of work.

- Who do you help?
- How do you help consumers and clients?
- What problems do you solve for them, and why is that significant?
- Share your purpose and goals.
- Discuss the impact you're making in your community. Tell about the transformations you make that help people look and feel better.

Consumers love doing business with people, not companies. They want to know who is behind your business. Show them your facility, your team, and your expertise.

Some of the biggest mistakes I see in positioning are:

- Not having a welcome video on the home pageof your website.
- Using young adult stock images instead of real pictures of the target market.
- No invitation to opt-in and get engaged with the brand.
- No articles, blogs, or video tips to educate consumers.
- No call to action or offers to join the community.
- Low pricing and too many discounts.

PRICING AND POSITIONING

Your prices have a lot to do with your positioning. You can position yourself as a low-end medical spa through pricing, at a level like Walmart. Or you can choose to offer medium pricing, such as Target, or you can be like Saks Fifth Avenue or Bergdorf Goodman and charge more.

Your positioning determines who you attract. Do you want to attract the affluent, or do you want to be the least expensive place in town? You can be either.

- Higher prices – you see fewer clients but earn more.
- Lower pricing – you see more clients, work harder, and make less.

My advice is to choose the first option, higher pricing. Let the competition play the price war games. You don't want to play that game because there's always some fool willing to charge less. Let them fight over scraps.

Make a decision now regarding your positioning and the type of consumers you want to attract. And begin by working on your position statement.

POSITIONING STATEMENT TEMPLATE AND FORMULA

A positioning statement is a short, structured sentence that explains who your company is and who you're talking to. It explains what sets you apart and why someone should choose you.

The components of a positioning statement:

- Target audience
- What you offer
- How you offer it
- Why cosumers should trust you
- How you compare to others—differentiation and key strengths
- Your commitment to providing excellent experiences

> *Through branding and positioning, you can make it easy for consumers to know that you are the only choice for medical aesthetics.*
> —Dori Soukup

Let your positioning statement be the foundation for your brand's personality, voice, image, appeal, and expertise.

SAMPLE POSITIONING STATEMENTS

Medical aesthetics: The XYZ Medspa is for people who care about their appearance, wellness, and health. They lead in offering the most innovative, result-driven treatments and products. They are dedicated to having a team of professional experts who deliver great experiences in a beautiful environment that is professional and welcoming!

Disney: To children of all ages, The Walt Disney Company, together with its subsidiaries and affiliates, is a leading diversified international family entertainment and media enterprise that serves to entertain, inform and inspire people around the globe through the power of unparalleled storytelling, because we believe in the power of exploration, happiness, and magical experiences.

Apple: For individuals who want the best personal computer or mobile device, Apple leads the technology industry with the most innovative products. Apple emphasizes technological research and advancement and takes an innovative approach to business best practices — it considers the impact our products and processes have on its customers and the planet.

YOUR MESSAGE, YOUR VOICE, AND YOUR WORDS

As a business owner, leader, marketing manager, or provider, you often find yourself sitting in front of a computer to write. It may be an email blast, ads, website content, newsletters, social media posts, or something else. Knowing how to write great content and defining your message is essential to your success.

Are you a good copywriter? Do you track the effectiveness of your messages, your words, and your conversion rate from your marketing efforts?

Most people find writing good copy to be challenging. Why do I say that? Because most of the content I see for menus, websites, and articles requires editing or rewriting. Keep reading and apply the following eight-step structure to improve your copywriting skills.

EIGHT STEP STRUCTURE TO WRITE GREAT COPY - IMAGE AND WORDS MATTER

This eight-step structure will benefit most of the copy you want to write. However, please note that this applies to copywriting for marketing your medspa or spa business, not for writing a book. For help on how to write a book, go to BecomePublished.com.

1. Headline – point out the pain point

The first step is your headline or, as I like to call it, the "hook." You must have a headline that grabs people's attention so they will keep reading.

A hook can be a pain point, or it may present a problem that people are seeking a solution to. You might present it as a question.

EXAMPLES OF A HEADLINE AND HOOK

- Want to make your acne disappear, but not sure how?
- Do you want to lose 20 pounds in 20 days?
- How can you make lines and wrinkles disappear?
- Is your skin feeling dry, flaky, and dull?

Take the problems that consumers have and create hooks out of them. Each one can be an entire marketing campaign.

2. **Subheading – the name of the solution**

The subheading should name the answer to the problem. Usually, it should be the name of the treatment that solves the problem you are addressing.

Example:

Headline: Do you want to lose 20 pounds in 20 days?

Subheading: Experience the XYZ weight-loss program and get back into your skinny jeans in 20 days.

The subheading should cause your consumers to keep reading.

3. **Benefits**

Describe the results of the program or treatment you'll provide. This is where you will discuss benefits.

Be careful not to go into the features. People don't buy features; they buy results, solutions, and benefits. You want to describe how they will feel once they lose 20 pounds. Connect with them on an emotional level.

Use bullet points for benefits because it makes them easier to read.

Example:

- Be healthier and have more energy with IV therapy.
- Increase your confidence level by having blemish-free skin.
- Look better in clothes and feel sexy with physician's weight program.
- Have silky smooth skin by ditching the razor and getting a laser.

4. **Proof that your treatment or program works**

Your proof is a testimonial that states how you helped someone else achieve results. It can be a video testimonial, a written comment, or a case study. You want to instill confidence that the treatment or product you are recommending works. The testimonials should overcome any objections a person might have. Make it easy for people to see that you are the right choice for them.

5. **Make an offer and have a call to action**

The offer is key. It must be enticing enough to grab your consumers' attention and entice them to take action now. Your offer can include added value, a gift with purchase, a complimentary enhancement, or a gift card. It should be something that creates urgency for them to purchase now.

Call to action

This is where you tell your consumers and readers what they must do to take advantage of your offer and get started. Your call to action may ask them to:

- Click a link to reserve.
- Call or text to purchase.
- Fill out and submit a registration.
- Take an assessment.
- Or something else.

Create something that causes people to take immediate action and do what you want them to do.

6. **Urgency**

You must create urgency. Urgency ensures they don't move on and leave your page without taking action. You want them to take action NOW.

Your offer must include an end date or a timeframe in which the offer expires. Or create an offer, perhaps, that's only valid for the first 25 people who reply. Urgency is about acting NOW to convert consumers into clients with your words.

7. **Promo codes and contact info**

Promo codes are essential for tracking your marketing campaign efforts and success rate. Your guest relations team must ask callers for the promo code so they can track it in the medspa software system. When a person calls about a particular offer, that needs to be noted in the system.

Be sure to include your contact information in all your marketing materials. Believe it or not, people often forget to include their contact information.

Following these eight steps will increase your marketing conversion rate tremendously. The more you write, the better you will become. Let the power of words work for you and enjoy your success.

The best advice I can give is always to do things that help improve your positioning in your community. Become an influencer, show your expertise, make a positive impact, support a local charity, speak, write, and be the go-to person for health, wellness, and It does take commitment, action, and desire. You have to want to be the best—the expert in whatyou do. Doing all these things will help you differentiate your business and crush the competition.

TAKEAWAYS

_____

_____

_____

_____

_____

_____

_____

SHORTCUTS TO SUCCESS

- Assess your online presence.
- Build a website that works for you.
- Brand yourself, your team, and the business as professional experts.
- Improve your copywriting skills.

INSPARATION MANAGEMENT BUSINESS TOOLS

- Brewing Brilliance Marketing Series.

CHAPTER 5

Gain Celebrity Status and Differentiate Your Business with Video Marketing

> *Marketing is no longer about the stuff that you make, but about the stories that you tell with videos.*
> —Seth Godin

I started filming videos about 12 years ago before anyone in the industry was doing them. Video marketing is one of the easiest ways to gain celebrity status, improve your positioning, and expand your outreach.

We have been teaching members and clients to film videos for years. Videos are the easiest way to make a name for yourself and show differentiation.

Let's go back to the example of your prospects searching online for treatments or products to help them rejuvenate. They'll come across many websites, articles, videos, and blogs, and Instagram, Facebook, and LinkedIn posts, and more in their search. The question is: are they finding you? And if they are, are you capturing their attention? Are they engaged, do they take action, and are you turning them into a lead?

Using videos helps you increase your chances of being found online. It captures consumers' attention and lets you showcase your expertise.

Next to text message marketing, marketing yourself and your business with videos is one of the most effective marketing strategies.

VIDEO STATISTICS

Here are some statistics about videos to get you excited and make you aware of the potential:

- Internet users consume up to 16 hours of digital video per week.
- 66% of consumers prefer to watch a video than read about a product.
- 68% of marketers say video has a better return on investment than Google Ads.
- According to Forbes, YouTube has the best Return on Investment (ROI) for video content, followed by Facebook and Instagram.

YouTube is the second most-used website on the planet, only behind Google. It has over a billion users. One-third of all people alive watch videos on YouTube. When someone is searching for something, they turn to Google and YouTube. Seventy-eight percent of people watch online videos every week. Fifty-five percent of people watch videos every day.

That alone should be enough to make you want to post videos online.

Three-quarters of each video is watched 65 percent of the time. Therefore, your videos need to

be short and exciting. Do short videos, a minute to a minute and a half. Product launches and treatment education tips are perfect for this length. Keeping them short increases the number of people who will watch your entire videos.

Go to YouTube and search for videos on Botox, fillers, CoolSculpting, facials, and peels in your city. Is your competition making videos? Most likely, you won't find any. It will be very easy for you to stand out, capture a more significant share of the market, and gain celebrity status.

When consumers find your videos, they will be drawn to you and not your competition. If everyone on your team showcases their expertise in online videos, your reputation within your community will rise.

If your competition does post videos online, that's all the more reason to start posting your own videos.

Many people prefer watching videos on their phone rather than on their computers. The average viewing session is more than 40 minutes, an increase of more than 50 percent from last year. Additionally, 300 hours of videos are uploaded to YouTube per minute. That's mind-boggling.

If your medspa is not using video marketing, you're missing out on massive opportunities to generate more leads and convert them into clients.

Videos are currently the best way to market your business because more and more people are watching videos.

Note to team members: Depending on your position within the medspa, be sure to gain management approval before creating and publishing videos. Adhere to the medspa's policy regarding video marketing. Even if you're recording it on their behalf, you're representing the company you work for. Know that videos are the property of the company. If you terminate your relations, those videos belong to the company.

Note to business owners: Make sure you put out team guidelines about publishing videos. If you allow the team to publish videos, make sure your medical spa name is included within the video, so it's clear who the video belongs to. Be sure everyone signs a video release form that gives you permission to post the videos anywhere online.

BENEFITS OF VIDEO MARKETING

Videos are one of my favorite methods to market, and there are many benefits to publishing videos. InSPAration Management's YouTube channel has hundreds of videos. Videos helped build InSPAration Management into a very successful and award-winning consulting firm.

We gain more leads from YouTube than any other marketing source. Not many of my competitors do videos as we do. We focus on video marketing, which is why we built a video studio in the corporate office.

> *If we did all the things we are capable of doing, we would literally astound ourselves.*
> —Thomas A. Edison

Professionals like you search for medical aesthetics business coaching and consulting. They find my videos, watch the videos, and realize we can help their business. They call the office for help. We set up a Success Planning session to discover their business challenges, and we offer solutions! You do the same thing with the consultation process. Go to InSPArationMangement.com to reserve.

The fact is that consumers are attracted to experts. When consumers search for what you do and see your video demonstrations and explanations of the transformations you deliver, they are much more likely to contact you and reserve a consultation.

Videos allow your business to stand out from the competition. When you don't have videos, you are like everyone else, and there's no major differentiation in positioning. Most of the competition does not post videos that demonstrate and explain the treatments they offer. Nor about anything else, for that matter.

Gain a competitive advantage by publishing videos. You'll improve your positioning, educate consumers about your treatments and products, build trust, and gain clients.

TYPES OF VIDEOS YOU CAN PUBLISH

- **Product videos**

For product videos, you can stand in your boutique, hold a face cream, and do a product video about it. A product video can be less than one minute. It should highlight the problem people have and explain why this cream is a great solution. It should include where they can get it and state your offer or added value.

You can have an entire product video library, which you can post everywhere online, that informs your community about your products and how you can help.

- **Treatment videos**

You can highlight each treatment on your menu and post a short video about it on your website. Film a brief description of what the treatment is, who it's ideal for, what benefit they'll see, and the expected results. Then invite the viewer to reserve a consultation.

Every page of your website should contain videos regarding the treatment featured on that page. That will make your website more engaging and help consumers realize how you can transform their appearance and help them reach their goals.

- **Educational videos**

Educate consumers by providing video tips. You could do a Tip of the Week. It's a great way to show your expertise and help educate your community. You can discuss the types of treatments available, both so they are informed and also so they see you and your team as experts.

You can do consumer tips on subjects such as maintaining a youthful appearance, how to exfoliate between facials, how important it is to get a peel, when to have a peel, and many others. The topics are endless. Create a shortlist and begin recording.

- **Video testimonials**

Ask your clients for video testimonials. We have more than 100 video testimonials of people like you sharing their experience with InSPAration. Video testimonials are worth millions. It's much better to have other people say how great you are and toot your horn, rather than you doing it.

If someone can't do a video for you, you can describe their success story, show before and after pictures within a video, and share their written testimonial. Chapter 7 further discusses the importance of video testimonials and reviews.

VIDEO STRUCTURE

Before we dive into video structure, I'd like to remind you why you are doing videos. The purpose is to capture consumers' attention, educate, engage, and convert them into leads and clients. You do this by having a good call to action within each video.

Remember that you're making videos because you want to be noticed and found online as the expert to gain celebrity status.

A six-step video structure applies to most videos:

1. **A hook, or attention-grabbing intro**

The same strategy described in the copywriting chapter applies to videos—you must have a hook to grab someone's attention. To create hooks, identify all the concerns people come to you for, make a video for each, and share the solution.

The concern is your video's intro and "the hook." You only have a few seconds to grab someone's attention. Start with the concern they're searching for.

Your intro can start with this type of hook: "Tired of fine lines and wrinkles? We help you make them disappear."

2. **Introduce yourself**

Introduce yourself after the hook.

"Hi, I'm Dori Soukup, an expert nurse injector at XYZ Medspa. I'm here to share the different options you have to erase fine lines and wrinkles and regain your youthful appearance."

3. **Offer the solution**

Describe the solution. "The most popular non-invasive treatments that give you a more youthful appearance are Botox and fillers. Botox and fillers are [speak about the benefits, and results]." Describe how they will feel about the results and the outcome.

4. **Proof the treatment is effective**

Your videos can give social proof that the recommendation works and produces results. Some viewers may be skeptical about specific treatments you offer, such as CoolSculpting, PRP, HydraFacials, etc. Address a viewer's skepticism through success stories and with before and after pictures.

You might start the video by asking, "Does CoolScupting really work? What is freezing your fat anyway?" And then state the reasons it does work.

This approach is very effective. You identify an objection a viewer may have and prove it wrong. You can address any doubts about the solutions you offer, then share a success story that adds further proof. The more social proof you provide about the success of this treatment, the fewer objections consumers will have and the more treatments they will purchase.

You may be the person that changes a viewer's mindset from skepticism to belief, all in a single video. The eyes don't lie. If viewers physically see how a treatment provides solutions and works, they will be convinced that the treatment is legitimate.

It's important to share social proof because some people doubt treatments are effective. Many people think claims such as "You'll look 10 years younger" sound too good to be true. They need to see physical proof to realize your treatments can indeed make them look 10 years younger.

5. **The offer**

It's critical to make an offer that entices a viewer with its added value. The offer could include a gift with purchase, an enhancement, a gift card, or something else that adds value. Decide what your offer should be before you start filming.

6. **Call to action and urgency**

Once you present the offer, include a call to action. A call to action should take a consumer to a landing page where they can learn more about your video's topic and take advantage of the offer.

The call to action may be "Go to xxx.com/injections to 1) Reserve a consultation, 2) Buy something, and 3) RSVP for a Botox party!" Then take them to the landing page where you describe the offer in more detail, and they can register or take another necessary action.

Be sure to indicate exactly what you want the viewer to do next. Tell them if they need to call in, click a link to buy, click a link to reserve, text to a certain number, or something else. Tell them what to do. Fail to present a call to action, and your viewers won't know what to do and will simply click away. A great "offer and a call to action" make a huge difference in the conversion rate and effectiveness of your videos.

Creating a sense of urgency prevents people from procrastinating. People like to put things off, but if you present a special offer, such as "the first 30 people to reserve a treatment get X," or you put an ending date on an offer, they're more likely to act quickly by taking action. Tie your offer to acting now. Create urgency.

Follow this video structure, and you'll create outstanding and effective videos. Feel free to mix it up some, but keep in mind that the structure presented here provides a solid foundation on how to film effective videos—ones that will convert leads into clients and position yourself and your team as experts.

Remember to keep your target market in mind and speak as though you are speaking to one person. Be sure to smile, look your best, and have a clear message. Refrain from being too stiff. Have fun! Let your personality shine through and enjoy yourself.

TOOLS FOR CREATING VIDEOS

You can start with a minimal investment. All you need is a phone or video recorder, a tripod, a microphone, a ring light, and a teleprompter for your phone (if you need it). You'll need editing software and someone to assist you. If you have a bigger budget, you can have a backdrop or a branding wall. Set up a company YouTube channel. Remember, this channel is for the business, not for personal use.

Once all the tools are available, start creating videos. You don't have to make a big investment in a studio, as we did.

The Brewing Brilliance studio in our corporate office is where we film all the videos and shows to help professionals like you succeed more. We built it to improve online learning and deliver better quality videos to all members and the InSPAration Management community. It's where we produce the Meet The Experts show, Dori Talks, and all the other educational programs we offer on Med Spa Biz University, the private member platform where all business tools are made available.

PUBLISHING YOUR VIDEO ON YOUTUBE

Your first step is to post your videos on YouTube. All your videos should be on YouTube.

Once you upload your videos there, you'll need to market them. Share your videos to all your online platforms: Facebook, Instagram, LinkedIn, Twitter, your website's interior pages, landing pages, and your newsletter. Put them in an email.

That's the beautiful thing about creating videos. It allows you to film one video, publish it on multiple platforms, and gain more benefits from one effort.

We invite you to subscribe to the InSPAration Management YouTube channel. You'll get to see how we do videos, our thumbnails, and how we title and post them. Also, read the documentation under each video so you know how to optimize videos for consumer searches and gain more viewers.

Make sure your video's title includes the treatment name and the benefit of the treatment. Also, include your city in the description. That will put your video at the top of local search results when people search for solutions to their problems in your area.

Below a YouTube video, you can include links to your website or landing page. That makes it easy for people to visit your website, learn more, and opt-in.

Get started by making a shoot list. Then begin filming and publishing your videos. Have fun, and begin generating leads while improving your positioning.

What do we want you to take away from this chapter? Committing to improving your positioning, showcasing your expertise, differentiating yourself, and gaining celebrity status by creating videos. Video marketing will help you accomplish your goals in the fastest way possible. It's super easy, and YouTube is free. Do it now. Ready, set, FILM!

We also invite you to subscribe to the InSPAration Management YouTube channel and ring the notification bell.

TAKEAWAYS

_____

_____

_____

_____

_____

_____

SHORTCUTS TO SUCCESS

- Set up your company's YouTube channel.
- Gather or purchase the filming tools you need.
- Choose your editing software.
- Create a video shoot list.
- Practice filming.
- Publish on YouTube.
- Measure effectiveness.

INSPARATION MANAGEMENT BUSINESS TOOLS

- Reserve access to the Brewing Brilliance studio for special interviews and filming.
- Apply to be featured on the *Meet The Experts* show.

    MeetTheExperts.com

CHAPTER 6

INCREASE REVENUE WITH ECONOMICAL MARKETING STRATEGIES

> *Master the topic, the message, and the delivery.*
> —Steve Jobs

Marketing is the responsibility of everyone on the team. This chapter will discuss self-marketing, cross-marketing, and referral marketing. These are the most underutilized strategies within a medical aesthetic practice, despite being the most effective and economical strategies. As Seth Godin said, "Word of mouth is all that matters."

Practice these simple yet very effective marketing strategies, and you will:

- Be more productive and help more clients achieve their goals.
- Operate at maximum capacity during working hours.
- Increase your client base.
- Generate more revenue for your business.

- Generate more income for providers.
- Fulfill and exceed the promise of your marketing and sales messages.

No matter what position or role you have, whether you are a CEO, founder, or provider, you can apply these strategies and philosophies to help you reach a higher level of success.

UNDERSTANDING CAPACITY AND KNOWING YOUR MAXIMUM POTENTIAL

There are two capacities to monitor. One is space capacity, and the second is team capacity. It's important to monitor both and always strive to improve them.

1. **Space capacity**

An average medical spa is about 1,500 square feet. It should include a reception area, where retail products are usually displayed, three treatment rooms, a consultation suite, a manager's office, and a team's lounge.

As an owner, you need to know how much revenue this location can generate daily, weekly, monthly, and annually. Forecast the maximum revenue potential at full capacity by knowing how much each treatment room can generate and how many clients you need on average per day to reach that goal.

When you know these two numbers, set your goals for maximum achievement. Think Big. Don't limit yourself.

Consider your team. How many hours does each employee work per week? How much would they generate from treatments and retail revenue if you operated at maximum capacity? How many clients do they need to reach that goal? Knowing the number of clients required per day is essential to reaching your goal.

Once you calculate your maximum capacity potential based on your space, use the following marketing strategies to map out your path to success and realize the true potential for the team and the owner.

We have a tool to help. We are offering you the Revenue Capacity Calculator, a preformatted Excel spreadsheet to help you determine your capacity and revenue potential.

Simply fill in the yellow cells, and you'll see your potential. Download the Revenue Capacity Calculator at InSPArationManagement.com.

2. **Team capacity – productive vs. non-productive time**

Every day, your team members get up, go to work, and stay there for eight hours. They can either operate at maximum capacity, being very productive by seeing one client after another, or just be there all day, seeing maybe three clients and operating at very low capacity. It's what we call "productive time vs. non-productive time."

A team member is getting paid an hourly rate, so he or she may be happy to float along, but their low productivity may have the business in a negative cash flow situation. The owner is paying them for non-productive hours. A business cannot thrive if it's paying its team a high hourly rate to sit around and be non-productive.

CALCULATE THE TEAM'S CAPACITY AND THEIR PRODUCTIVITY RATE

To be a high achiever, you need to commit to being productive and reach for your maximum potential. Practice self-marketing to increase your productivity and reach a higher level of success.

Set goals for the number of new clients you'd like to gain each month: retention rate, number of self-generated clients, number of referrals, and cross-marketing opportunities. Remember: don't just set achievable goals; stretch and aim higher.

SHIFTING THE PHILOSOPHY ON SELF-MARKETING

When we train teams on-site, we see that most team members drop the ball on self-marketing, cross-marketing, and referral marketing because they think it's the owner's responsibility to market the business. They think owners should simply roll out the red carpet so they can show up to work and receive their silver platter with all the clients they need.

It doesn't work that way.

It's a challenge in the industry, and in fact, most team members do not practice self-marketing, cross-market, or ask for referrals. Why not?

Because they weren't ever taught a systematic way to do it. Nor do they have the right marketing tools to do it effectively.

Lastly, there are no expectations or measurement systems for their performance.

These are the most common reasons that most medical spas operate at less than 50 percent of their capacity.

When we consult with clients about their team's effort to market, we often hear: "The team is not motivated to do anything. They aren't helping. They lack drive, contribution, and dedication to success. They just want to show up, do the work, and go home. Everyone wants success, but some are not willing to work for it."

The industry is in need of a mindset shift regarding whose responsibility it is to market the business. It's everyone's responsibility to market and promote the medical aesthetic clinic, no matter their position. Word of mouth is all that matters. The entire team must be proactive and practice this mindset.

> **Don't wait for your ship to come in, swim out to it!**
> —Steve Southerland

High achievers go the extra mile to help others and help themselves. Don't be the person who waits for his or her ship to come in. Nobody wants one of those people on their team.

You want to be an A-player. A superstar. Be the proactive type. Do what is unexpected. Surprise people with your great efforts. Have a positive impact and fulfill your purpose.

TOOLS YOU NEED FOR SELF-MARKETING, CROSS-MARKETING, AND REFERRAL MARKETING

- Business cards
- Medspa dollars
- Gifts cards
- Referral cards and forms
- Offers
- Landing pages for opt-ins
- Social media platforms
- The menu
- Scripts for team training

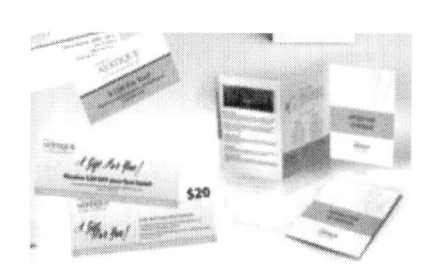

SELF-MARKET WITH BUSINESS CARDS

Your business card is a very economical marketing strategy to help you self-market and gain new clients. We're not talking about a typical business card.

Create a business card that includes a gift offer on the back, perhaps $25 to $50, depending on your pricing. The idea is to have them reserve a consultation and apply that gift to a customized program worth thousands of dollars.

BACK OF BUSINESS CARD OFFER

Notice it's NOT an offer of 10 percent or 20 percent off. Twenty-percent-off fillers are a considerable discount. It's a gift card with a dollar amount off. An injector offering a $50 gift card to be applied toward a first filler treatment makes a much less costly offer. It's classier and different. You'll attract new clients and earn more.

It's easy to self-market and generate new clients when you're out in your community. You always see new people at the grocery store, bank, mall, church, Starbucks, etc. There are many opportunities to communicate with people, make new friends, and gain new clients.

Most people have about 250 connections in their network. There are endless opportunities to self-market and self-generate new clients each day!

THE 3-FOOT RULE AND HOW TO USE IT

Here is an easy technique you can use when you're out in public.

When you get within three feet of someone who fits your client profile, make eye contact and smile. When they return the smile, you can say hi and compliment them on something you notice. Make sure it's sincere. Start a conversation, and people usually ask, "What do you do?"

Make sure you have a mini-commercial prepared so you can answer that question well. Write out a short paragraph that explains what you do.

Mini-commercial example: "I'm an expert nurse injector. I work at XYZ Medspa and perform medical aesthetic treatments. For the past five years, I've been helping people look younger and feel better about themselves. I love my work!" Then ask them what they do.

Another example: "I'm an aesthetician. I work at XYZ Medspa, and I specialize in medical facials. What do you specialize in?" Saying, "I specialize in..." is a great approach.

You can add, "I help people like you have beautiful and younger-looking skin through treatments and products." Always ask next, "What do you do?" Then hand them your business card with the gift card offer on the back.

Never say, "I am just a...." You're not *just* anything, and those words should never come out of your mouth. I hear it from people all the time because most don't view themselves as experts. Remember, you are an expert.

As you're saying your mini-commercial, people will form an opinion of you. Make sure you come up with a good one, practice it repeatedly, and start using it.

> **Give gifts first, receive second!**
> —Dori Soukup

OFFER A GIFT WHEN SELF-MARKETING AND BUILD RELATIONSHIPS

Remember that you're having a conversation with a new friend. They ask you what you do, you ask them what they do, and then before you go your separate ways, you can say, "It was so nice to meet you. Here, I'd love to give you a gift!"

Hand them your business card, gift side up, and say, "I'd love to invite you to stop by. I can show you around, and if you see something you like, you can use the $50 gift card toward your first treatment!"

The business card should have the offer: "A Gift For You!" Receive a complimentary consultation and a $50 gift card for your first visit at XYZ MedSpa."

Include a QR Code that takes them to a landing page where they can opt-in and redeem it. Or include a number where they can text GIFT to opt-in to your mobile list and redeem it, if you practice text message marketing.

This strategy transforms your plain old business card into a self-generating business opportunity. Instead of just handing people a business card, you give them a card with a gift. That makes a huge difference in gaining self-generated clients.

Practice this process, be genuine and professional, and tap into the infinite possibilities within your reach. Make it a habit!

Set a goal to hand out at least five cards per day and never stop. Keep meeting people and making connections. It's a smart strategy, and even if only one person accepts your offer, your capacity and income will increase.

Get those cards ready, begin self-marketing, and start generating new clients you can help.

SELF-MARKET ON SOCIAL MEDIA PLATFORMS

Self-marketing on social media is the Wild Wild West. Currently, most businesses don't have very detailed social media policies.

As a business owner, make sure your social media policies and guidelines are very clear to your team. They must know that clients belong to the business and not them. Therefore, when they promote their work on social media, it must be along with the business name, not just under their name as an individual.

To avoid misunderstandings, place business watermarks on all your images, so the public knows they belong to the business.

Provide the team with guidelines for your approval process, such as who's allowed to post on the business page and how to post on their personal pages.

Encourage the team to create content for social media, but make sure they know your policies and guidelines. Include these in your employee manual.

Make sure everyone signs an authorization form and remember to adhere to HIPAA laws.

Be mindful of using personal social media accounts to self-generate clients. Potential clients may make assumptions about your business based on a social media account, especially if that account includes sensitive content. It might be best to only post on the business's social media account in such a case.

Everyone has a choice as to which career path they take. If you choose to be an employee, you must respect the business's policies and be ethical. If you cannot do that, you should work on your own. You should always practice an excellent work ethic as a team member.

We hear many stories of nurse injectors who work in medi spas and decide to move across the street, open a place, and take all the clients along. That kind of behavior is unacceptable. It's critical to be upfront and honest with your goals and efforts. Being dishonest and deceiving will always come back to haunt you.

Social media can be a great place to self-market and lead new consumers to the medspa and you. There are some real rockstar injectors who know how to market themselves and gain thousands of followers.

One of my favorite self-marketers (and much more) is Shelby Miller from Ruma Aesthetics in Utah. Shelby is a friend and client with more than 100,000 followers on Instagram. (Her Instagram handle is Aesthetic_injector). She started out working for someone else, became a solopreneur, and now has one of Utah's most successful medical spas. She also does one-on-one clinical training to help others improve their clinical skills. Shelby has amazing talent, and she is a high achiever. The key to her success? She takes action and does the work.

If you choose to self-market on social media, know the parameters and always act professionally.

PRACTICE SELF-MARKETING

Be confident when you're self-marketing to prospects. If you're meek and shy, you must overcome it. Simply smiling more will attract people to you. Start communicating with people and practice being approachable.

Always look professional. You won't be successful at self-marketing if your hair is wrapped up in a bun, or you have no makeup on, and you're wearing wrinkled clothes. It seems obvious, but not everyone realizes this. The last thing you want is to self-market or display your business name when you don't look the part. After all, we're in the beauty business.

Make sure you always look great, even on your days off. You're always self-marketing and self-generating clients, so always look good and be ready to meet new people.

As a business owner, set key performance indicator (KPI) targets and give your team bonuses based on the number of self-generated and other referrals they receive each month.

INCREASE CAPACITY AND PRODUCTIVITY WITH REFERRALS

> *You can double your business if each client refers just one person.*
> —Dori Soukup

It's easy to ask for referrals from existing clients and double your business. The problem is that teams usually don't ask. Usually, we discover the team has no targets, no goals, and no consequences for not asking and gaining referrals. Remember to always ask, and you shall receive!

The number of referrals you gain directly reflects your retention rate and the type of experience you deliver. If people enjoy their experience with you, like and trust you, and love their results, they will refer clients to you. All you need to do is ask.

REFERRAL MARKETING

Here's how to start asking for referrals.

First, shift your mindset. How many clients do you treat each day? How many of those clients could refer someone to you? Set a goal for the number of referrals you want to generate per day, week, and month. Reaching those goals will improve your business, income, and capacity.

The best time to ask for referrals is after you've exceeded someone's expectations.

The myth: many people think it's necessary to pay someone who gives you a referral, but that's not the case. Deliver terrific experiences with great results, and people will love referring others to you. All you do is ask.

If you have a loyalty program, you can reward the referring client by depositing points into their loyalty account, which they can redeem toward treatments or gifts. But don't give cash. It's viewed as fee-splitting and is illegal.

Here's an example of how to ask for a referral:

"Beth, you've been a loyal client for a while, and I love taking care of your treatments. Is there anything we can be doing to enhance your experience even more?"

Let them tell you yes or no. If the client says, "Yes, there is something you can do to enhance the experience," then find out what and make it better.

If they say, "No, you're doing great," continue with the rest of the script:

"Thank you, Beth! I could use your help. I have a couple of openings in my schedule, and I'd love to fill them with people like you." You're telling your client how much you appreciate her.

"Who do you know that would benefit from the treatments we provide? Maybe friends, family, colleagues? Who can you think of?" She will usually tell you.

Then tell her: "We can send them an invitation with a special gift card to visit us, via email or text. Would you be so kind as to share their contact information?"

Thank your client for helping you, and get the contact info, so you can follow up on the referral and make sure they use the gift card.

Note: Make sure you inform the guest relations team to place a message in the software system saying it's your referral.

Use this strategy at the end of each treatment to generate referrals, increase your capacity, and earn more money.

Remember to keep notes in your software system about which clients you ask for referrals because the last thing you want is to be annoying and ask the same people every single time. If you asked at the last visit and they didn't offer a referral, you may want to bring it up lightly or skip it until the next time.

Note: Make promotional gift cards a certain color that's only used for gift card promotions. Those gift cards should not be filled with money in your system, or they'll show as a liability on the P&L statement, and you don't want that. The color will help you know that there's no money on the card and that it's for marketing only. When a client redeems one, simply apply a credit on their account and note in your system that the referral card was applied.

Promotional gift cards are totally different than gift cards people purchase. If they buy a gift card, of course you put money on it and process it through the system. But do not process promotional gift cards until you are ready to apply them toward a treatment and then do it as a credit or discount.

GAIN MORE CLIENTS WITH A REFERRAL CAMPAIGN

You can launch a referral campaign and promote it for one or two months. The campaign can say, "Refer a friend, and you both have a chance to win a $500 gift card!"

Everybody on the team should wear buttons stating, "Win a $500 gift card. Ask me how?"

Have registration cards for clients to list their name and the name of their referral. Have these cards everywhere. Every time a client provides another referral, put their name in the running for another opportunity to win $500. Make sure they aren't referring people who are already clients. You want new prospects.

The great thing about this campaign is that you're only giving away two $250 cards—one for the person who refers and one for the referred person. It will cost you $500 to run this campaign, but you'll generate hundreds of referrals. It's a great strategy!

If you need more help with this, contact InSPAration Management and we'll be happy to help you plan an entire campaign. You can create posters, flyers, postcards, emails, social media posts, and buttons to properly promote the campaign, so you generate as many referrals as possible.

Note: Make sure you have a system to process referral leads immediately. Generating leads is one thing, converting them to a consultation and a client is another. Have a post-campaign strategy that ensures a high conversion rate from all registrations.

CROSS-PROMOTING STRATEGIES

This is the easiest type of marketing strategy to implement. When we visit clients on location, we sometimes hear their clients say, "Oh, I didn't know you did hair restoration," or "I didn't know you have laser hair removal," or the same about CoolSculpting.

When we hear that, we know the team is not cross-marketing. Cross-promoting marketing is amazing when the entire team participates by promoting each other.

Cross-promoting is made easy with the Daily Success

Planning (DSP) meeting and when you use medspa dollars.

I mentioned DSP meetings in a previous chapter.

Morning or shift meetings are held to discuss which clients are visiting your facility that day. It's also the time to identify opportunities to gain referrals, to cross-promote, and to discuss the delivery of great guest experiences.

The Daily Success Planning meeting lets every team member become familiar with all the clients visiting so they can recommend treatments that other team members can perform.

Of course, that takes some research into the history and types of treatments your clients have had to inform the team how they can best help.

CROSS-MARKETING USING THE MEDSPA DOLLAR

Let's say Beth is a regular client who frequents the medspa, but she only receives Botox. She has not experienced any other treatments.

At the end of her Botox treatment, you can give Beth a medspa dollar and say, "Beth, you've been coming to us for a while, and I always love doing your Botox. I was looking in your profile today, and I noticed you've never had a Hydrafacial here. Have you ever had one? You know, it's the facial that the stars have for the red carpet. It literally makes your skin glow. I want to do something special for you. I actually have a gift for you to thank you for your loyalty."

Show her the medspa dollar with the offer. "Your gift is $25, and you can apply it toward your first Hydrafacial. I want to introduce you to Melissa. She is an absolutely amazing medical aesthetician. We can go ahead and apply the medspa dollar toward your first facial. That way, I can take care of your injectables, and Melissa can help you with the texture of your skin and make sure it stays healthy and glowing."

Do your fact-finding before the Daily Success Planning meetings. Who is coming in, and what treatments have they had in the past? What opportunities do you have to help your clients achieve better results by cross-marketing?

Applying this strategy will help you increase patient/guest satisfaction, generate more revenue, and increase your capacity. Always have medspa dollars in the treatment rooms, ready to use.

Imagine a team that discusses who's visiting, who's going to cross-market to whom based on what treatments they've previously had, and which treatments they'll benefit from. That will make the entire team busier, help the clients by providing more options, and generate more revenue.

Every medical spa, spa, medical practice, and wellness center that implemented the Daily Success Planning meetings has seen major improvements overnight. You can, too, but you must commit to hosting your DSP meeting daily. It makes such a difference with the guest experience and productivity.

CROSS MARKETING AND TEAM CREDIBILITY

When cross-marketing, it's important to know your teammates, their expertise, and their credibility. It's wise to create a team credibility and expertise binder or an electronic file that everyone can access to learn about their teammates so they can speak highly of each other.

When you introduce a teammate, use words such as "amazing," "an expert," and "the best." Say, "people drive for miles to see her," and "her clients love the results she helps them achieve." Build them up.

Say, "We can set up a consultation for you and let her customize an entire treatment plan that will best benefit you. Let's go ahead and take care of that for you!" If you do that regularly, the entire team will be much better off, and so will your clients.

Know one another, know everyone's role and strengths, and build each other up, so you can cross-market with confidence and take advantage of all the opportunities you have each day.

RESERVE THEIR NEXT APPOINTMENT

Cross-marketing is useless if you don't make an appointment. Don't hesitate, reserve the appointment right away. Take them to the reception desk and have them reserve it right on the spot.

Say, "I want to help you. Let's go ahead and reserve your complimentary consultation, where Laura can help you choose the ideal facial, and then you'll be able to apply this offer." If the aesthetician is available, introduce the client. If not, attempt to book the client's next appointment.

If they refuse to take advantage of the medspa dollar, say, "No worries, just keep it in mind. Maybe next time you come, you might want to schedule the facial back-to-back with your Botox so that we can take even better care of you."

If you don't ask, you won't receive. You must attempt. You must make an effort.

> *The secret to marketing success is no secret at all. Word of mouth is all that matters.*
> —Seth Godin

TURN NON-PRODUCTIVE TIME INTO PRODUCTIVE TIME

There are only so many hours in a day, but you can take your non-productive time and turn it into opportunities where you make more money and are much happier.

If you have empty blocks in your schedule, ask yourself, "How can I get busier and be more productive today?" Look at your teammates' schedules and see if you can educate their clients on what you do. Or, if you can, provide them a sample treatment, this will help to introduce them to what you do.

That increases the likelihood of receiving more opportunities. Ask yourself, "Which client can I offer complimentary mini-treatments to"? and make them an offer.

If you're not doing this, you're being average. You're not seizing opportunities that are right in front of you. Take your non-productive time and convert it to cross-marketing opportunities via mini-treatments that you do for someone while they have other treatments. That's how you increase your capacity.

Implement these marketing strategies to self-generate clients. They're very easy to implement. Just remember, set your goals. Practice the script and the approach. Role-play and put your own personality into it. Then start doing the strategies and measure your performance.

TAKEAWAYS

_____

_____

_____

_____

_____

_____

_____

SHORTCUTS TO SUCCESS

- Assess your current efforts regarding the three marketing strategies (cross-marketing, self-marketing, and referral marketing).
- Customize your scripts and implement the three strategies.
- Create marketing materials.
- Set your goals and targets.
- Determine your Key Performance Indicator (KPI) bonuses.
- Plan Daily Success Planning (DSP) meetings.

INSPARATION MANAGEMENT BUSINESS TOOLS

- Recipes for Success Team Training Modules on Med Spa Biz University.

CHAPTER 7

ELEVATE YOUR SUCCESS WITH REVIEWS AND TESTIMONIALS

> *Reviews and testimonials will help you become the obvious and only choice for consumers.*
> —Dori Soukup

As the world changes, consumers also change the way they use technology within the buying process. Reviews and testimonials are powerful marketing strategies, every medical aesthetic must practice them to influence buying decisions.

Imagine this scenario: You're planning to have dinner with friends at a restaurant you've never been to before. What do you do? You get out your phone and search it on Google. You go to their website to see their menu, pictures, and ambiance. Then the next step is to look at their reviews, right?

The reviews will help you determine if you want to eat there or not.

You base your decision on what other people have said, and you are not alone.

- 90% of consumers read online reviews before visiting a business.
- 88% of consumers trust online reviews as much as personal recommendations.
- 72% of consumers say positive reviews and testimonials make them trust your facility more.
- 63% of consumers say that they are likely to check online reviews on Google before visiting a business.

If these statistics don't encourage you to gain more social proof with reviews and testimonials, I don't know what will. If you want to work smarter, work less, and have more consumers visit you, start asking for reviews and testimonials.

What I described above is the new decision-buying process. Whether someone's looking for medical spa treatments, furniture, books, makeup, skincare, or cars, all consumers do it.

Focusing on gaining reviews and testimonials must be a marketing priority for you and the business. Reviews are essential to your success, so I'm dedicating a whole chapter to this topic.

When planning your strategies on how to gain more recognition for what you and your team do, it's important to understand two things: What consumers look for in reviews and testimonials and how a business benefits from reviews and testimonials.

1. **What consumers look for in reviews and testimonials**

- That you are a professional medical spa.

- That they will be spending their money on quality treatments and products.
- That you have experts and skilled employees and teams.
- Guest satisfaction—what other clients experienced and whether they were happy with the results.
- The number of stars you've received and whether people recommend you.

2. **How a business benefits from reviews and testimonials**

- They provide social proof that you are experts in what you do.
- You appear in searches, which expands your brand's online reach.
- They solidify your brand as a professional medical spa.
- They help feature you as experts and the best and only choice.
- They help you generate more leads and make more sales.
- You discover ways to improve your guest experience.
- They help you convert more prospects into clients and overcome objections.

Obviously, there are many benefits for both consumers and businesses. I encourage you to apply the strategies in this chapter to maximize their benefits to your business.

DIFFERENCES BETWEEN TESTIMONIALS AND REVIEWS

Testimonials are statements you request and collect from clients after they do business with you. They're usually from clients who already know you and come to you for treatments and products. Testimonials can be spoken, presented on audio, written in a guestbook, or videotaped. My favorite, and most effective ones, are video testimonials.

For example, at the end of each seminar we host—whether it's the LEAP Ahead Seminar, the Millionaires' Circle, the Mastermind Group, or the Write Your Book in One Weekend Seminar – my videographer always asks attendees to provide video testimonials on the spot.

Go to the InSPAration Management's YouTube channel, and you'll see more than 100 video testimonials. It's very strong social proof that helps your clients choose you. See how we do it and then do the same. Subscribe to our YouTube channel while you're there, and you'll receive notifications when we publish future videos.

Reviews usually consist of online statements or comments that describe someone's experience with you or the medical spa, good or bad. Reviews usually aren't provided to you in-person, they are normally posted online.

After I spoke at the Aesthetic Conference in Las Vegas, a doctor came up and asked if I would look at his website and give my opinion. One of the first things I noticed was that someone had linked his Yelp reviews to his website's homepage, and the very first review was only one-star. I couldn't believe my eyes.

He was investing money in Google Ads to drive people to his website, only for prospects to get there and see a one-star review. What a great way to shoot yourself in the foot.

Linking reviews from another platform to your website can do more harm than good if the reviews aren't good. Always monitor and control the content that appears on your website. You can always post great reviews there yourself, but don't have them link automatically unless all your reviews are between 4.7 and 5 stars.

Reviews and testimonials are some of the most economical marketing strategies you can practice. After all, everybody is constantly on their phone searching for things. They're searching for facials, Botox, fillers, CoolSculpting, and massages, and the competition is fierce. Many places offer the same treatments.

But reviews and testimonials give you the competitive edge and help determine who they will choose.

If reviews are lousy, you're keeping people from coming to you and your business. If reviews are great, you just exponentially increased your rate of conversion from prospect to client.

The goal of reviews and testimonials is to help convince consumers that you are the best choice.

Reviews and testimonials are extremely powerful tools to help you succeed, so commit to asking for them. They'll help you improve your reputation and your positioning. They'll set you apart.

Excellent reviews will help crush your competition.

GOALS FOR REVIEWS AND TESTIMONIALS

Set targets and goals for how many reviews and testimonials you want to receive per day, week, and month. To help you calculate your goals, determine how many clients you see on average per day and then what percentage of them you want to provide testimonials and reviews. Do you want to capture reviews or testimonials from 20 percent of your clients? Or 40 percent? Set your goal and go for it.

SEVEN STEPS TO MAKING REVIEWS AND TESTIMONIALS WORK FOR YOU

1. **Deliver a great guest experience**

When you deliver a "wow" guest experience, and go beyond what's expected, you create raving fans who notice your efforts. When your guest experience is fulfilling and exceeds expectations, you won't need to do much convincing to gain reviews. Some will even do it on their own.

The point is that if you want reviews and praise, make sure everyone on the team is delivering a great guest experience and then ask guests to give you reviews.

You can have the most beautiful spa, but if clients don't feel welcome and you don't provide a "wow" guest experience, they will just feel like a number and probably write a bad review.

Everyone on the team has a big responsibility to gain positive feedback and reviews. Make sure the entire team is committed and trained to deliver a great guest experience.

2. **Set up a business profile on review sites**

You want reviews on the most popular review sites. Start by setting up your profiles on the sites you want to guide people to. I recommend doing so in this order:

- **Google** is the number one website for reviews. Ask your clients to leave reviews on Google more than anywhere else.

- **Yelp** (some clients have told us they do not recommend paying for Yelp's services).

- **TripAdvisor** is especially significant if you're part of a resort spa, destination spa, or medical tourism.

- **Other social media sites**. Ask your clients to share comments with their friends, connections, and followers. Ask them to leave reviews on your company's social media platforms. Decide where you want them to go and create your profiles.

3. **Make it easier to ask with review cards**

Create business-sized review cards for your team and clients to make the process easier. The card can state: "Your thoughts are important to us; please share them. Tell us about your experience."

Print the cards and make them available for the guest relations team and all providers to use. Train the team on how to use them, set targets, and make it a habit to use the cards to ask for reviews.

Include your Google review account, Facebook account, YouTube account, and Instagram. Wherever you want them to leave a review, guide them there.

MAKE TESTIMONIALS EASY WITH A GUESTBOOK

Another way to gain reviews and testimonials is via a guestbook. Purchase some nice leather-bound guestbooks and at the end of each treatment, ask people to write a note about their experience so you can build a library of glowing testimonials.

These leather-bound books should be all over your facility, so people can easily read and write testimonials. They will demonstrate your expertise and guest satisfaction.

TESTIMONIALS MADE EASY WITH VIDEO SET-UP

We went into detail about video marketing in Chapter 5. Now, I'd like to tell you how to make it easier to get video testimonials.

Set up a specific spot in your facility for video testimonials. Have it up and ready all the time, and then ask as many ideal people as possible to give you a raving video testimonial.

That's very important. Clients who implement this strategy have increased their testimonials by 1000 percent.

A video camera setup allows the team to record testimonials easily. You'll be amazed how many people love to give testimonials when there's a camera, and then you can share them everywhere.

VIDEO TESTIMONIAL STRUCTURE

Guide your clients on giving you a testimonial by asking them to tell a story about the two of you.

- They searched for a solution to a problem and found you.
- Have them talk about the treatments and experience they had.
- Ask them to describe the results they achieved.
- Ask if they will highly recommend you on camera.

They can tell a story using those points. Tell them to speak from the heart! You helped them look good, and now they're helping you by singing your praises.

Note: Make sure all clients sign a social media release form, and your employees. This will ensure you avoid any legal situations. It will keep you from inadvertently violating any HIPAA laws.

The social media release form must be part of the initial paperwork you ask clients to sign before receiving treatments. Always remind clients that their testimonial will be used on social media and other websites, both when they first sign the form and before filming the testimonial.

4. **When and how to ask for reviews and testimonials**

The best time to ask for reviews and testimonials is at the end of the experience when you've impressed them. Or, if you are doing a head-to-toe consultation and customizing a program for someone, you can offer incentives to gain reviews and testimonials once the treatments are complete. Of course, if they had an invasive treatment, wait until their "after" photos to ask for a testimonial.

Most people will agree to provide you with a testimonial, while only a few will refuse. All you need to do is ask, but if you don't ask, you will never receive any testimonials.

If the client is open to doing a video testimonial, that's great. Take them out to the lobby and do it. Go over the points described above.

Note: Avoid asking, "How was everything?" Instead, ask, "What was your favorite part of your experience?" "What did you like best about your experience?" "Oh great, please tell me more!" Always ask open-ended questions.

If they don't want to do a video testimonial, respond, "No problem, maybe you can write a note." Show them the guestbook, give them a pen, and encourage them to write a testimonial about how great their experience was.

When someone offers a compliment, ask, "Would you be so kind as to say exactly that either on video or in the guestbook?" They already told you, "I loved my experience, and this was my favorite part." Now they'll just write it down or say it in front of the camera.

When we go on-site for a secret shopper mission and training, no one asks us to provide a testimonial. You'll immediately stand out from the competition if you make it a habit. Once you set your goal, keep that goal alive, and obtain as many reviews as possible.

PREPARE THE CLIENT FOR A TESTIMONIAL

Help your clients look their best while giving you a video testimonial. Don't record after you've taken their makeup off, and obviously, not after an invasive treatment. Set up an appointment for their "after" pictures and a video testimonial.

Only ask for video testimonials when your clients look their best. You want them to feel confident about their appearance as they give the testimonial. You want to show off members of your community and how good they look.

5. **Say 'thank you'**

Always, always say thank you immediately after someone gives a testimonial or review. You can set up an automated message thanking them as soon as you receive a review.

I recommend setting up a Google Alert that notifies you every time someone mentions your name or the company name. That will let you acknowledge them immediately.

Go to "Google.com/alerts" and type your name and then your business's name into the box. Anytime Google spots someone mentioning you or your place, you'll receive an email, and you can respond to the comment right away.

It's critical to monitor all testimonials and reviews you receive and make sure you address them accordingly.

6. **Post your testimonials and reviews**

When you receive written testimonials and online reviews, post them everywhere to gain more exposure and show your followers and community how you're making a difference in people's lives.

You can also take the online review and write it in your testimonial book. You can put it on your website, Facebook, Instagram, LinkedIn, newsletter, your medspa's digital loop, and anywhere else.

7. **Train the team, measure, and repeat**

Anytime you implement something new, it requires planning your process, creating the tools, scripts, and system, and training the team.

Once you roll out the new plan, it's important to set standards, goals, and how you'll measure performance. Train, measure, improve, and repeat.

USE REVIEWS AND TESTIMONIALS TO GENERATE SALES AND OVERCOME OBJECTIONS

A client may hesitate to receive a certain treatment because they aren't convinced it's effective. Showing them other people's testimonials and reviews about that treatment may convince them to go ahead.

If a prospect tells you, "I don't know if I'm ready for fillers right now," you can say, "You remind me of Nancy. She said the same thing, but here's how she feels now that she had the treatment."

Identify the objections you usually receive from people. Obtain testimonials that help you address those objections so that you can overcome them with ease and with stories. Most objections can be overcome with social proof.

Testimonials generate more sales when you use them as stories to inform people it's okay to do something new. They give consumers confidence in what you do and how great you are at doing it. Testimonials are an extremely powerful tool that convince people to say "yes" to what you're recommending.

If someone doubts you or hesitates to receive a treatment, just open your guestbook full of testimonials, or show them the online page where other people who had that same treatment state how happy they are now.

Build a library of testimonials and reviews, use it to help you generate more sales and position yourself as the expert you are. Organize reviews by treatment types electronically, or in a book, or both.

MANAGING NEGATIVE REVIEWS

Everyone gets a bad review here and there, and it's not the end of the world. I've seen plastic surgeons make huge mistakes with terrible reviews and even lawsuits, and they're still practicing.

Of course, you never want it to go that far. The point is that there's a way to manage bad reviews but do it offline, not online.

Here's the process to manage bad reviews:

- Respond promptly.
- Write like a person, not a corporation. Empathize with the client.
- Take it offline – do not go back and forth online.
- Provide options that will make it right.
- Deliver on your promise.
- Follow up to ensure the client is happy.

What do you do when you get a bad review? Respond right away. Assign a person who is responsible for monitoring your online reputation and have guidelines on how to respond.

Keep an eye on notifications and address bad reviews as soon as they show up.

Don't air your dirty laundry in public. The only thing you need to say is, "We are so sorry to hear about your experience. Please contact us to see how we can help."

That way, if anybody sees the bad review, they see you as a company that tried to make it better. That's all they need to see.

Never fully address what the reviewer says online. Be very careful, especially if you have a medical spa, as there are HIPAA laws you could violate by being too specific.

Ask them to contact you so you can address their situation. Give them a call, apologize, find out what happened, and then make it better if you can.

If you can fix their problem and make them feel better, ask, "Would you be so kind as to please remove the bad review now that we've helped you get exactly what you need?" Make sure they remove it.

The best way to overcome bad reviews is by having many good reviews to counter the bad ones. That's why you should ask for reviews and testimonials as often as possible, so you can get as many good reviews and testimonials as possible. Then you won't worry about one bad review.

If somebody sees that you have 500 great reviews and only two or three bad reviews, they'll know you're a good company. If you have two or three bad reviews and no good ones, you need to take immediate action to get some good ones.

I'm often asked: "Should we pay people to give us reviews or testimonials?" My answer to that is, no, don't pay. When people love you, trust you, and you know you're doing great by them, they'll want to help you. That's just human nature.

But if you're not treating them well or providing the results they want and not giving them love and attention, then you don't deserve them, and they'll go somewhere else.

Again, know exactly how many reviews and testimonials you want per month, set that goal, and ask for them. People will give them to you. Many people will say yes to starring in a testimonial.

Remember to rehearse the script. Train how to ask for reviews and testimonials. Role-play the approach so your words come out smoothly and with confidence. Start measuring to see how many reviews and testimonials you receive daily.

Then, use your testimonials to sell and market to your community. You'll be able to overcome many objections and reach a higher level of success.

TAKEAWAYS

_____

_____

_____

_____

_____

_____

_____

SHORTCUTS TO SUCCESS

- Identify platforms for your reviews.
- Purchase a few quality guestbooks for written testimonials.
- Set up your video camera and backdrop for video testimonials.
- Train the team on how to ask for reviews and testimonials.
- Set goals for the numbers you'd like to reach.
- Build your social proof library and use it to differentiate your business and overcome objections.
- Organize your reviews and testimonials electronically and in book format.

INSPARATION MANAGEMENT BUSINESS TOOLS

- Private team training webinars
- Recipes for Success Volumes I, II, III, and IV.

Part Three
The Guest Experience and Retention

CHAPTER 8

FIVE STEPS TO A SUCCESSFUL LIFETIME CLIENT JOURNEY

> *Whatever you do, do it well. Do it so well that when people see you do it, they will want to come back and see you do it again, and they will want to bring others and show them how well you do what you do.*
> – Walt Disney

A key factor for growth and business success is defining a client journey that converts new guests into lifetime clients. Yet many practices don't emphasize the client journey. Most don't even know how many new clients they receive per month, let alone what happens with them.

That's a strong statement, but it's true. When we work with new clients, the first step is assessing their business model. Often, we find they're missing a client journey process.

Turning high numbers of new guests into lifetime clients requires a system, strategies, training, and tools. The journey is not always very clear to the business owner or team.

In this chapter, I share the InSPAration Management business model we help clients with, so you too can implement a terrific new client journey that turns new clients into lifetime ones.

VALUE OF A LIFETIME CLIENT

Let's begin by defining what lifetime clients are and how to calculate their value.

Lifetime Value (LTV) estimates **the average revenue a client invests in their personal improvement over their lifespan with you**.

According to marketing consultant Philip Kotler, "a profitable client is a person, household, or company that, over time, yields a revenue stream that exceeds by an acceptable amount the company's cost stream of attracting, selling, and servicing the customer."

HOW TO CALCULATE YOUR CLIENT'S LIFETIME VALUE

Run historical client and revenue reports for the past few years.

- How much is each person spending with you?
- How often do they visit?
- What's the average amount they spend per visit and annually?
- What's the overall retention rate?
- How many years do they remain clients on average?

Example

- Average revenue per client visit: $1,000

- At six visits per year, average annual revenue: $6,000
- Retention period (five years): $30,000
- 20% profit margin (five years): $6,000

The lifetime value calculation is determined by **multiplying the value of the client to the business by their average lifespan**. It tells you how much revenue you can expect to generate and profit from each client over the life of their relationship with your company.

Knowing this number also helps you determine how much you can invest in acquiring a client and still be profitable. The longer you retain them, the lower your client acquisition cost.

Take the time to calculate and study these numbers. If you are just getting started in business, you'll need to forecast your financials. Look at your business plan and set your targets and budget guidance.

Explain this to the team, so everyone knows the value of each client and how critical it is to turn them into lifetime clients instead of only one visit and they're gone.

We'd all rather generate $30,000 than $1,000. And that amount doesn't take into consideration other revenue opportunities and relationship benefits, such as annual average retail sales, the number of referrals they bring you, and reviews that help you generate more leads.

Calculate the value of your current clients and set goals to elevate your success.

BECOME THE DIRECTOR OF YOUR LIFETIME CLIENT JOURNEY

Do you like watching plays or movies? Most people like both because they tell stories. Each story has a script, actors, and an audience.

Picture your client's journey as a play or movie. It has characters, each with their own role. There are team characters and client characters. Team characters have their scripts, and clients have their challenges. In the story, you discover what the clients' challenges are, script out how you help them solve those challenges, and forecast their outcome.

Is it a happy story? Is it a story that the client wants to stay in as the hero, or do they leave and never come back? Did you kill them off?

You are the director of this play. As director, you need a clear story, scripts, casts, sets, lights, cameras, and action to engineer and orchestrate this play. What is your client journey, and is it leading to long-lasting roles?

Simple enough, right? It can be when you implement the InSPAration Management business model that we teach. It's super effective and outlines the entire client journey from their first visit to becoming a lasting character in a soap opera that never leaves.

The journey usually begins with someone searching and finding you. Once they find you, they see your brand, information, research skills, and expertise. Your role is to grab their attention and entice them with an offer that encourages them to join your community or at least ask for more information.

To impress them, you must have attention-grabbing content and a professional image. You are much more likely to capture someone's attention, generate a lead, and turn them into a prospect when you have that.

You can use all sorts of marketing strategies to generate new prospects.

- Online presence on your website, social media, YouTube, LinkedIn, and elsewhere

- Gift cards
- Referrals by other clients
- Marketing campaigns
- Walk-ins
- Events where current clients are invited to bring a friend
- B2B referrals, and much more

Check out the Marketing for Success plan, where you will find more than 70 marketing strategies to help you generate new leads and prospects.

LIFETIME CLIENT JOURNEY

01 Marketing Generate Qualified Leads – Marketing Department

02 The Lead Opt-in Or Incoming Management Calls – Guest Relations – Contact Center

03 Reserving A Get To Know Journey – Guest Relations – Contact Center

04 "Get To Know You" Consultation. Customize a program – Treatment & Product Specialist

05 Begin Their Program, Deliver A Great Experience – Treatment Providers – Guest Relations

06 Monitor Experience & Results – Treatment Providers – Survey

07 Enrollment Journey Into The VIP Program – Provider Team & Guest Relations

08 Relations To Lifetime Client – Entire Team

Five steps to a successful lifetime client journey

As you begin to plan and direct your "play," you'll want to assign a role to each part or character of the journey. The post opt-in process is a huge part of the client journey success.

STEP 1. LEAD MANAGEMENT AND POST OPT-IN ENGAGEMENT

Whose role is it? Guest Relations

Your guest relations team needs to adopt a new philosophy regarding leads and prospects. Prospects are the air that a business needs to breathe. If the phone isn't ringing with new prospect inquiries, the business will flatline and vanish sooner or later. The guest relations team must understand the importance of lead management and what their role is within the client journey.

The Guest Relations role

Manage incoming leads and prospects.

- Check daily for new prospects coming into your sales funnel.
- Determine if they are new or existing clients.
- Put new clients in the system.
- Contact the prospect via phone, email, or text, and thank them for inquiring.
- Confirm what they are looking for.

When working with clients and assessing their lead management processes, we often find hundreds of new prospects in Mailchimp or Constant Contact, just sitting there with no one paying attention to them. If you make the guest relations team responsible for monitoring opt-in and all new inquiries, that won't happen. All leads must be processed and taken through the journey.

The outcome

When the team is trained on lead management and is playing its role well, you'll ensure every lead and prospect is worked properly. By doing this, you're helping to fulfill your purpose. Applying roles helps you gain more new clients that you can convert into lifetime clients.

STEP 2. GIVE FIRST, THEN INVITE THEM FOR A VISIT

To be effective in the second step of the client journey, you need engagement. Offering a gift will help you make a great impression. Then invite the prospect or lead for a visit to begin building a great relationship.

Ideas for effective gifts and offers for leads and prospects

Provide a "first visit" gift card.

- Invite clients for tea and cookies and a "get to know each other" experience.
- Depending on their inquiry, reserve a treatment at the same time as the "get to know each other" visit.
- Reserve a time for them to visit.

Whose role is it? Guest Relations

It's the responsibility of the guest relations team to invite a new lead and reserve their first visit. The goal is to convert them from a prospect to a first-time visitor. Arm the team with the strategy and tools to convert at a high rate.

Note: To increase your conversion rate, we recommend doing a fact-finding exercise to learn more about each prospect. Go on Google, research their name, and note your findings in your software system. Include their profession, lifestyle, social status, and hobbies. Are they an influencer in the community? You can do that in a couple of minutes. Keep it professional.

Note: If you're an InSPAration Management member, you have access to guest relations videos and the training manual, which contains scripts on converting leads into new guests. They are available on Medspa Biz University.

The outcome

When you have a lead management process and train your guest relations team on its role and parts in the client journey, you'll improve the guest experience and tremendously increase your conversion rate.

Set a goal for the number of "get to know each other" visits you want the team to reserve per day, week, and month, so you can help as many consumers in the community as possible, monitor performance, and keep improving your conversion rate.

STEP 3. THE "GET TO KNOW EACH OTHER" EXPERIENCE

View the first visit as a first date. You want to make a great, lasting first impression, so make the visit special. Invite the prospect for tea and cookies, and make it warm and inviting like two friends having afternoon tea and discussing the latest and greatest methods and treatments to look great. Sit in a living room-style consultation suite or at a round table. Avoid a desk with you on one side and them on the other. That's not how you sit with friends.

That first visit is to connect, show credibility, build trust, discover their concerns, needs, and wants, and make recommendations. They should walk away with a professional customized treatment and product program that outlines all the options to help them look and feel their best.

Note: During the Daily Success Planning meeting, the guest relations team must let everyone know what new clients will visit that day, so they can meet them, welcome them, and play their assigned role accordingly.

Whose role is it? Treatment and product specialists or providers

This part is usually played by a consultant, or what we like to call Treatment and Product Specialists (TPS). Alternately, it may be a provider, depending on your business and organizational structure.

Ideally, we recommend having a specific "Get To Know You" (GTKY) consultation department with defined roles that performs all new client consultations. You want one person to focus on this part of the journey. An employee taking on more "characters" or roles in the same play creates confusion for the team and clients, hurting the production. We believe in having one or two people play this role and conduct all consultations.

Clients who implement this model generate six figures worth of new revenue per month.

Treatment and product specialist role

The TPS role is to perform the GTKY journey and convert new prospects into clients with a customized program that helps them and gains them as clients. An entire process and system are needed to conduct this first date/first visit journey, so you both benefit and create a win-win relationship.

Again, this experience should be as comfortable as two friends getting together and discussing ways to look and feel better. It should be as comfortable a setting as a room in your home. Please, no desks.

Through conversation and the use of an intake form, the TPS discovers:

- What they want to improve or enhance.
- What will make them happier?
- How can you help?
- What solutions are available?
- What are their expectations?
- What are the expected results?

To make this experience fun, educational, and engaging, it's important to let the client express their thoughts. Always use a beautiful, hand-held, magnified mirror. Have in front of you an intake form or, as we like to call it, the Get To Know You form.

The form must include a list of the problems and concerns people usually have with their face, body, wellness, and sexual health, and the solutions you have in your menu of treatments.

Make it easy to complete by including simple statements with checkboxes:

- I have saggy skin.
- I have hyperpigmentation.
- I have large pores.
- I have fine lines and wrinkles.

They will go down the list and check off all their concerns.

If you don't explore and don't use the Get to Know You form, it will feel more like selling. You might come across as pushy, and you don't want that.

The GTKY form opens the door to discussing all their concerns. Listen, understand, and then help them by customizing treatments and creating a products program. Present all the options to them.

Remember that, via your menu, concerns equal solutions.

Example of a conversation: "You've expressed your concerns and goals during our conversation, and the good news is that we can definitely help you achieve great results. Here's what it will take."

Then go over the customized program you've created to help them, explaining the process. Tell them it will take more than one treatment to achieve their goals.

"Mary, if you're serious about addressing these concerns you shared with me and seeing the changes, you'll need to go through this customized program. It includes a range of treatments and products to help you achieve the results you're looking for."

This is easily implemented with the Success with Guest Consultations program and the S.A.C.R.E.D. system. That program outlines all the steps needed for the team to perform the Get to Know Each Other journey successfully.

The outcome

Performing a Get to Know You visit will allow you to customize programs that best help your clients and let you generate high-ticket $4,000 to $10,000-plus from each consultation. Clients get better results, and you increase capacity and revenue.

It will take you away from what I call the first visit a la carte business model everyone operates under to the one we developed, prove most successful, and that I'm sharing with you here.

A-LA-CARTE ➤ VS. ◀ CUSTOMIZED PROGRAMS

> *Minimize the a la carte process & shift to the Get To Know You Consultation System, and grow your business exponentially.*
> —Dori Soukup

STEP 4. DELIVER ON THE PROMISE—TREATMENTS, EXPERIENCE, AND RESULTS

Now that they're a new client and you've determined a customized program, it's time to deliver on your promise. The quality of their treatment experience with you and your brand will determine whether they become a lifetime client or not.

Whose role is it? All providers—the entire team

Providers and Guest Relations must be committed to delivering great experiences.

How do you define a great experience? A great experience is when the client leaves your business saying, "Wow! That was amazing!"

When did you have your last "wow" experience? Sometimes there are good experiences, but truthfully there's room for improvement in the service industry. That makes it easier for you to deliver that "wow" experience because many people are often disappointed everywhere else.

Go beyond people's expectations and turn them into lifetime clients that come back to you again and again.

It takes training and practice to deliver a "wow" experience. The more you practice, the more skilled you will be. Pay attention to the details: Your place must be spotless, organized, and have a great scent. The entire team must look great and be well-trained, highly skilled experts.

When you stand out positively, you rise above the rest.

What are the provider's roles within the client journey?

The client experience starts from the moment they set foot in the facility. It's how you greet them, take them into your treatment room, deliver their treatments, the recommendations you make, the tools you use, and the protocols—all the processes you go through. It all needs to be planned and orchestrated so that every time a client visits, they have an outstanding experience.

Delivering a great experience helps you retain more clients and charge higher prices. A high-quality hotel like the Ritz-Carlton trains its employees very well. They constantly provide great experiences, and that's why they can charge high fees. Deliver a great guest experience, and people will keep coming back, no matter how high your prices are.

The moment you step foot in your facility, you're on stage and need to perform. There's a psychological effect that happens when people first see you based on your aura and positivity. Be warm, joyful, sincere, and confident. Clients love dealing with confident people. All those factors determine how likely you'll gain them as a lifetime client.

The outcome

When you follow a system—a strategy—to deliver a "wow" guest experience, you will see consistency, accuracy, and growth in your business.

STEP 5. THE CLIENT'S JOURNEY INTO THE VIP MEMBER PROGRAM

In Chapter 12, we'll discuss how to create a model of recurring revenue. Having a recurring revenue model is something we want everyone to implement. It's the best way to manage cash flow within your business and ensure success. It's something we practice in InSPAration Management, and it's a model we believe every medical spa should be practicing.

Whose role is it? It's the entire team's!

It's important to know when a guest is nearly done with their customized program, which may take two, three, or four months, or more. That's when you should explain your VIP program.

What's the team's role? To present the VIP program and enroll clients in it.

> *The secret to having lifetime clients, Is to deliver a great guest experience and offering a VIP membership with a recurring revenue model.*
> —Dori Soukup

Show them an option to protect their investment, maintain their results, and save money by becoming a VIP member.

The VIP program is ideal for everyone—the clients, the team, and the business. Your recurring revenue is automated and charged monthly. The client can choose any treatment within the price range of the amount they have banked, and in return they receive special pricing for being a member.

The outcome

The outcome is a valuable lifetime professional engagement.

Of course, there's a lot involved in implementing a client lifetime journey model, but I want to at least open your eyes to the opportunities most professionals do not maximize. I also want to remind you not to reinvent the wheel. There are models available that are easily implemented. I've outlined them under the Shortcuts to Success and the InSPAration Management business tools.

Excited about the opportunities? Start by assessing your current process and then create a new "play" as described above. Maybe expand, so you have a new cast filled with stars. Then rehearse and direct your successful play.

Your growth or business success formula is to continue generating prospects and delivering great experiences so that clients stay with you for at least five years.

Remember, since it's like directing a play, make it a good one. Define all the roles, establish the characters, and make it enjoyable for everyone to get involved.

TAKEAWAYS

SHORTCUTS TO SUCCESS

- Develop a new play to include the client lifetime journey.
- Define roles and characters.
- Train Guest Relations on lead management and the "Get to Know You" role.
- Train providers on the client journey, the play, and the roles and characters every person will perform.
- Create sets, get your place ready for a great experience, and determine the desired outcome.
- Develop and implement a VIP program with a recurring revenue model.
- Helpful tools to structure the entire client journey are the consultation, recurring revenue, and guest relations training to reserve GTKY sessions.
- Team training is critical.

INSPARATION MANAGEMENT BUSINESS TOOLS

- Success with Guest Consultation and the S.A.C.R.E.D. system
- A recurring revenue model with the C.O.P.I.E. system

CHAPTER 9

TOUCHPOINTS TO ENHANCE THE GUEST EXPERIENCE AND INCREASE RETENTION

> *The key is to set realistic customer expectations, and then not to just meet them, but to exceed them —preferably in unexpected and helpful ways.*
> —Sir Richard Branson

The medical aesthetic industry is growing rapidly, and there is no shortage of medical spas, so how does one gain market share? Some people fear competition. They see a new place open and start reducing their prices, thinking that will help them, but they're wrong.

The best way to compete is through the type of guest experience you deliver. Many companies, including huge brands, have succeeded and continue to succeed through the client journey experience.

When Howard Shultz started Starbucks, everyone thought he was crazy to charge $4 for a cup of coffee. But not Howard Shultz! He knew he was not selling coffee. He was selling the experience he found in Italy. Needless to say, we are paying even more now, and he's turned it into one of the most successful businesses. All from selling an experience, instead of a product or price.

Walt Disney had the vision to provide a great magical family experience. He turned his Disney parks into an essential part of the family vacation experience.

Then there's Steve Jobs and the Apple experience. While there are many cell phone brands, Steve Jobs talked about the Apple and Mac product experience. Apple never discounts its products. It only has one special per year, on Black Friday, when they give you a $100 gift card.

This is where skeptical people say, "But I'm not those companies." True, but you can still focus on making your experience be why people choose you.

The point is that you realize the type of guest experience you deliver is what makes your business grow and flourish—not your prices.

My advice is to turn client experience into your most significant competitive advantage, using touchpoints.

Here are some experience statistics and their impact on businesses from a Forbes study:

- 84% of companies that work to improve their client experience report an increase in revenue.
- 73% of companies that deliver an above-average client experience perform better financially than their competitors.
- 96% of clients say service is important in their choice of brand loyalty.

- Loyal clients are five times more likely to purchase again and four times more likely to refer a friend to the company.
- 70% of people have spent more money to do business with a company that offers great service.

Are you convinced that you should work on improving your guest experience? Great!

Let's talk about how to use touchpoints to improve your guest experience and increase retention.

WHAT ARE EXPERIENCE TOUCHPOINTS?

Experience touchpoints are where consumers and clients interact with your brand, product, or service. They are opportunities to impress and connect with consumers and clients. They are the little details that make the guest experience great.

There are three areas where you can insert special touchpoints to enhance the client journey experience.

1. Human touchpoints
2. Products and treatments
3. System touchpoints

Mastering touchpoints in the experiences you provide will give you a great competitive advantage.

HUMAN TOUCHPOINTS

Check-in touchpoints. What can you do to make your first impression unique? You can implement welcoming touchpoints at check-in.

An example would be your guest relations team providing essential oil-infused refreshing towels. If the weather's cold, offer a warm towel. When the weather is warm, provide a cold one. Wet the washcloths with water and a couple of drops of essential oils.

Those small washcloths or towels will leave a great first impression on your clients. It's the little details that count. They also provide you with an opportunity to promote your essential oils.

Delta Airlines does this in its first-class cabin. They always provide me with a hot scented washcloth before serving drinks or a meal, and I always like it. Your clients will, too.

At the mall, perfume counters hand out small-scented cards to entice people into buying their perfumes. You can do the same when people enter your facility.

Instead of having a refreshment bar with only water and coffee, offer a tea bar with fruits. Improving your refreshment bar and welcoming ritual will encourage people to arrive early and let you provide a "wow" experience.

Companies like White Lion provide private-label gourmet teas. They can set up a great bar for you, and you can sell the teas, too.

PRODUCT AND TREATMENT TOUCHPOINTS

Beauty bar products. I sometimes see retail products behind locked doors when visiting medical spas. That's not a good idea. Consider, instead, having a beauty bar where clients can touch, feel, and sample products, which makes them more likely to purchase.

Highlight a Product of the Month for your clients to sample. Your boutique can have areas for wellness, anti-aging, relaxation, and more. Perhaps you make recipe cards for each category. The recipe card will list all the products and treatments needed to address specific concerns.

Make it fun and engaging. You could have an electronic feature that informs consumers about each product and its benefits. Or shelf-talkers that inform about products, sampling opportunities, and video loops about your products. That will make your retail area come to life, and you will generate more sales.

TREATMENT SUITE TOUCHPOINTS

Your treatment suites must be pristine and prepared for each client. All beds and chairs must be perfect when the client enters the suite. If you're providing facials, make sure the room and the bed are beautifully prepared and not lumpy or bumpy. The towels must be clean and feel great.

Your treatment suite should look like the Ritz-Carlton. If the suite looks great and you make an exciting and professional presentation describing the treatment you'll be performing, you'll put your client at ease and help them enjoy the journey—even if it's uncomfortable.

There are many touchpoints you can do at the beginning of a treatment. You can start by centering the client. You can do breathing exercises with essential oils or relaxation exercises. Using Sprayology, you can give your clients a spray in the mouth for relaxation and a better experience. You can give them a chocolate kiss, use stress balls for more invasive treatments, or provide a huggable pillow. Use an enhancement card to choose more treatment options.

Other treatment welcoming rituals include handing the client lavender stems or daisies. You can provide a specialty drink of the month instead of water. The possibilities are endless.

Remember to change your welcoming ritual roughly once per month. Your clients will not be as impressed if you use the same welcoming treatment ritual month after month. Try to surprise current clients with new experiences as they become lifetime clients. Plan and script each welcome ritual for the team to learn.

Touchpoints enhance the experience and help you promote more of your products, which they can take home. You can do these rituals for any kind of medspa.

SYSTEM TOUCHPOINTS

System touchpoints, some of which can be automated, include everything from client pre-arrival forms to the online experience you provide and your online shop.

They include: how you reserve appointments, text messages, emails you send, and the notes you make about client preferences. Touchpoints can make the check-in and check-out process effortless and enjoyable. They include your documents, how you track your loyalty points, and the VIP program payment collection.

A professional image is critical for all your collateral material and marketing. Your forms must look professional, match your brand, and include proper disclaimers. Whether they are paper or paperless, make sure they look good.

Touchscreens, tablets, and laptops can hold your client surveys, upgrade options, and membership options. Be sure that everything you present has your company logo, colors, and branding. Everything must look consistent.

CHECK-OUT TOUCHPOINTS

Make the check-out process productive and fun. One touchpoint you can practice is to give your clients a positive Hay

House card when they leave (see hayhouse.com). Those are nice, small decks of cards with positive statements on them. Have them choose one card—it's a very nice touch.

Another touchpoint is to hand out a going-away gift. It could be a small organza bag of flower petals for the car or lingerie drawer. I encourage clients to use large glass urns and fill them with lavender, calendula, and rose petals. The employees ask the clients which scent they prefer and then put petals into a little mesh bag tied with a hang tag. It's a nice gift that keeps people's car or drawer smelling fresh. The extra gifts are unexpected and get the client to say, "Wow, this was very special!" It makes a huge difference and a lasting positive impression.

We love Sonoma Lavender (sonomalavender.com). They offer all sorts of great products you can use to enhance your touchpoints.

There are many things you can do to differentiate yourself from the competition. Even your branded bags and tissue paper make a great impression. Gather the team and brainstorm how and what you can do to improve your guest experience.

We emphasize five relationship principles to help build lasting professional relationships:

1. Respect. The entire team must practice respect for the client and each other.//

2. Addressing needs. Be helpful and offer solutions.

3. Respond positively. Take action.

4. Serve with passion. Fulfill your purpose.

5. Connect emotionally. Establish loyalty and spread happiness.

DESIGN AND DIRECT YOUR GUEST EXPERIENCE

Host a team meeting and brainstorm touchpoint ideas to deliver a "wow" experience. Clients want to be happy and feel better about their looks after seeing you. They want to feel important, so treat all your clients as VIPs. Your top clients should be treated like super-VIPs. Give every client true value. Do the unexpected and exceed their expectations.

Clients want to be impressed by your expertise. Offer innovative solutions and impress them with customized programs.

The Golden Rule says to "treat others as you would like to be treated," but I don't necessarily believe that.

I prefer the "Platinum Rule," which states, "Treat others as they would like to be treated." How you want to be treated by others may differ from how I want to be treated by others. Keep track in your software system of your clients' likes and dislikes, so you can treat each client the way they want to be treated. Know their preferences.

Determine each client's favorite treatment and record it in your software system. "Tracey loves aromatherapy." "Mary's favorite facial is the HydraFacial."

These notes will help you treat your clients exactly how they wish to be treated. Remembering their favorite treatments and products will impress them. They'll say, "Wow, I can't believe you remember that!"

Treating your clients exactly how they want to be treated is how you "wow" them. If you don't record people's likes and dislikes, you'll forget their preferences and deliver an indifferent experience for everyone. Live by the Platinum Rule: "Treat others as they would like to be treated."

Many high-end companies keep profiles of their clients. I'm working on my two million miles with Delta Airlines, and they know all my preferences. They do their best to accommodate me. The Ritz, or the Four Seasons Hotels, do the same for their frequent guests. Restaurants that I frequent, and even the team at Starbucks, know precisely how I like my coffee.

That's service. You and your team will set yourself apart if you do the same.

OPERATING AND COMMUNICATIONS GUIDELINES

Never use the phrase, "I can't do this or that," or "That's our policy."

If somebody asks you for something you can't do, say this instead: "Well, I can't do that, but here's what I can do." Things are not only black or white, but there is gray. Try not to bluntly refuse to do something. If you must, offer something else in its place.

Yes, it's important to follow your policies and procedures, but you should be able to satisfy consumer requests within certain guidelines. Be sure you're smiling and be kind as you explain what you can offer. Show some flexibility and attempt to satisfy your clients' requests—it will provide you with many lifetime clients who'll say, "Wow, you're a professional. You're always trying to help me. You're always doing the best for me."

Follow your policies and be flexible when you can.

VALUES AND PROFESSIONAL PHILOSOPHY

The late Tony Hsieh, CEO of Zappos, wrote the book *Delivering Happiness*, which describes how to "wow" guests and deliver a great guest experience. Zappos rates its customer service representatives based on how long they keep customers engaged instead of how fast they get the customer off the phone with a purchase.

Nordstrom is known for its customer service. One of its customer service stories involves a lady who bought some tires from a tire store. The lady decided to return the tires to Nordstrom, even though the store does not sell tires. Nordstrom let the woman return the tires to them. That's amazing customer service.

Nordstrom's customer service wraps your merchandise neatly, places it in a bag, and walks around the counter to hand it to you. They make their customers feel special with every purchase, even if it's just a pair of socks. Nordstrom will also mail a note saying how nice it was to meet and serve you.

Disney is another master of customer satisfaction, orchestrating the guest experience with grace and fun. Disney does a lot of planning and training to ensure a magical guest experience. The company also trains its employees to maintain consistent quality service. Every employee must consistently follow company values.

Paying attention to details is vital to creating a "wow" experience. Valets at the Ritz-Carlton and the Four Seasons look at your luggage tag and greet you by name. That makes guests feel special and welcomed. If there is no luggage tag, they ask for the guest's name right away. This small detail adds tremendous value to the guest experience.

Treat your guests as five-star companies treat theirs. Treat them as if they just stepped into a five-star hotel. Use formal and inviting language and exude a positive aura and energy. It's attention to detail and strong values that create five-star experiences.

You might be thinking, "But I don't work for the Ritz-Carlton." That's stinking thinking. You can either have class and deliver a great guest experience or a casual, average one. A professional and fun experience attracts affluent clients ready to invest with you.

Professional language should be your default. Say, "Ms. Client." If a client asks you to address them in a certain way, use the Platinum Rule to show flexibility and address them how they want to be addressed. Never use casual terms of endearment such as honey, baby, sweetie, or love. I suggest you record the next experience you provide to observe your current language. Make necessary adjustments.

You have choices: You can either be like the Ritz or a budget hotel. Which clients do you want to attract? Keep that in mind as you design your guest experience and touchpoints.

RECOVER FROM AN 'OOPS,' AND INCIDENT REPORTS

No matter how good or talented everyone is, you may have a problem within the guest experience. Problems could include burning a client with a laser, a sloppy injection, or an allergic reaction. Have protocols in place to address problems and always address them quickly and well. Then complete an incident report.

Do you have an incident report form? Are you taking statements and pictures, if applicable? Do clients sign consent forms before they start a treatment? Always protect yourself and your guests from unwanted situations.

Never sweep issues under the rug. If you don't address mistakes, your clients won't come back, and they'll also tell others about their experiences.

Assess your experiences and current touchpoints. What's working and what's not? If you aren't using any touchpoints, create some. I encourage you to implement some of the touchpoints mentioned here and create some of your own to go beyond your clients' expectations. Fulfill their needs, fix mistakes, and deliver a "wow" experience. When you do, you'll increase your retention rate and earn more. Remember, when you help others get what they want, you'll automatically get what you want.

TAKEAWAYS

_____
_____
_____
_____
_____
_____
_____

SHORTCUTS TO SUCCESS

- Assess your touchpoints.
- Design your guest experience.
- Train on all touchpoints and implement them.
- Direct your guest experience and your client journey.
- Survey your clients about their experiences.
- Design your guest experience with touchpoints.

INSPARATION MANAGEMENT BUSINESS TOOLS

- Branding material assessment
- Effective consent forms to protect your business
- Secret shopper to assess your guest experience

Part Four
Success Without Being Salesy

CHAPTER 10

FINANCIAL HEALTH – YOUR BUSINESS IN THE BLACK

> *"*
> ***To succeed in business, you must have an effective sales model.***
> *—Dori Soukup*
> *"*

Part Four will help you develop a financially healthy business and/or chart a professional career. You can be an owner or an employee. Either way, focusing on revenue generation is essential to your success.

Most often, what we see missing from the client journey we discussed in earlier chapters is a defined sales process. Within the client journey, there are opportunities for sales.

Yes, the sales process. Some people may be freaking out now. "Oh no, we're going to talk about sales"! That's right, I'm bringing up the word "sales," which is sometimes viewed as a dirty little word.

I'm not sure why, because no business survives without sales or revenue streams. Your medspa is not a non-profit organization. Revenue and profits are essential to having a healthy professional career or business. Imagine if not one sales transaction took place in the world today. What would happen to the entire financial economy? It would collapse.

So yes, sales and sales processes are key, and they require focus and effort.

WHAT IS A SALES PROCESS?

The sales process is a preplanned, defined sequence of steps taken to turn a lead into a paying client. It outlines every move from initial contact to sale and beyond. Every medical facility will benefit from having a defined sales process.

Fact: A lifetime client journey includes them buying from you! Money for services and products changes hands. That's how the world works.

Successful medical spas have a sales process that the team implements and practices every day. If you don't, here are some of the common challenges and mistakes you will experience.

MISTAKES TO AVOID

- Your business does not have a sales model, process, or system.
- You don't generate enough revenue or profit.
- You don't maximize the guest's number of treatments due to fear of selling.
- The team is not clear on the sales process, nor are they trained on it.
- The team does not understand the importance of generating revenue.
- The team does not know their part and their role.

- There are no clear goals by department, revenue stream, or person.
- There's no team buy-in.
- There's no focus on business training or mentoring.

There is some good news, though—some light at the end of the tunnel. We've seen many businesses succeed by implementing the following sales processes:

6 STEPS TO CREATING A SUCCESSFUL SALES PROCESS

1. Adopt a new sales process philosophy and mindset.
2. Develop a sales process and client journey.
3. Clarify the client sales journey and the team's role.
4. Gain buy-in (what's in it for you and guests).
5. Train your team on how to generate revenue and exceed goals.
6. Measure performance.

Start by assessing your current sales process. See how you can improve it by applying some of the models in this chapter. The client sales journey could include the following:

- **Awareness Phase.** They find you and become aware of what you offer; they have a problem, and you have a solution.
- **Interest Phase.** You pique their interest with a complimentary gift card.
- **Evaluation Phase.** You show your expertise, add value, and build trust.
- **Decision Phase.** You show why you are the best and only choice.

- **Purchase Phase.** They purchase from you.
- **Repurchase Phase.** They keep coming back and then become a member.

Those phases don't happen by themselves. It takes each team member understanding and performing their role within the sales process journey.

Easy? No. This is the biggest challenge we come across in my firm.

Sales and the mindset behind them are the big elephant in the room. That's where we see pushback when we try to implement success tools. No one wants to sell. It's often a major block and a dead end.

It takes a lot of effort to change people's mindset regarding sales from negative to positive. However, the good news is that some people change, buy in, and succeed!

Those are the high achievers.

> *This is a business. You are not playing house with expensive medical aesthetic toys for free.*
> —Dori Soukup

Business owners invest a large amount of money in equipment, furniture, training, teams, products, and marketing, and they need a return on those investments. Everyone on the team must play their part for everyone to succeed.

When the team buys-in on the sales process, the rest is easy. It's simply learning and applying an effective business model. At that point, your destination is success. But it does take a team rowing together, in the same direction, and applying the same efforts to reach that goal.

Remember, there is no "I" in "team." A team is a group of people that achieves more by working together. "Staff" refers to people who work within an organization but don't emphasize teamwork. Think about it—there are no "sports staffs," but only "sports teams."

Your facility must have a team mindset and not a staff mindset.

DEFINING THE SALES PROCESS

1. Adopt a new sales process philosophy

Adopting a new sales process philosophy requires a new way of understanding the current situation. As medical professionals, and/or maybe a new business owner or professional, you find yourself trying to make it because no one ever taught you how to run a business. They don't teach business principles in medical school, and that's why many medical aesthetic practices fail. They don't have a clear client journey sales model and process.

Of course, many people operate successful businesses, but only because they took the time to learn business principles and strategies.

In most cases, the current philosophy is, "I'm not a salesperson." You fight and resist making sales because you view selling as something bad. You don't want to push things on people. You're uncomfortable talking about or asking for money.

The good thing is that we teach a philosophy that allows you to generate revenue without being "salesy." Keep an open mind as you read this chapter.

'SELLING IS VERY SIMPLE'

When we ask seminar attendees, clients, and members why they decided to open a medical spa or why they work in the industry, the most common answer is "to help people."

Fulfilling that purpose and helping your clients requires you to make recommendations as to how they can address their concerns and reach their desired results.

Remember that revenue generation or sales, whatever you want to call it, is essential to your success. Without revenue, good cash flow management, and focusing on sales, you won't reach your goals.

We all wake up every morning and go to work. Why? Because we want to? Or is it because we need to earn a living? We have responsibilities. We need money to meet our financial obligations, live a nice lifestyle, and buy what we want when we want it.

Since you get paid for what you do, you're one of the business's expenses—therefore, you need to bring in a lot more revenue to compensate for what they pay you. If you don't generate revenue, you're not helping the business and won't be employed there long.

You must buy-in on the importance of generating revenue and contributing toward your success and that of the business.

I used to feel the same way you're probably feeling about the sales process. But when I was 19 years old, I met Jim. Jim was the best insurance salesman in the country. He'd just moved from California to Florida and worked at the resort where I worked. He took me under his wing and taught me to be a great salesperson. His message was so simple yet so effective. I've practiced it ever since.

He said, "Dori, selling is very simple. All you have to do is find a concern or problem someone has and offer a solution through your recommendations."

That one simple phrase can change your life like it changed mine.

Think about it. It's very profound and should remove all the fear you have about selling. In fact, forget selling. Simply discover a client's concerns and provide recommendations to address them via your menu. Voila!

The recommendations are your treatments and products. That's it.

Fact: Clients come to you because they have concerns and problems, they need your help with. All you need to do is make recommendations that help them achieve their goals. By making recommendations, they achieve their goals, and you succeed. That's how you can help them and yourself. That's how you succeed.

Don't think of it as selling. Think of it as fulfilling your professional obligation by making recommendations to help your clients. Do this with every guest, and you'll convert them into lifetime clients. Everyone wins.

2. **Clarify the guest's sales journey and the team's role in it**

Revenue generation is everyone's responsibility. No matter who you are or what position you hold, everyone should know how much revenue needs to be generated, and their share of the contribution. That should be in your position descriptions, the employee manual, and all your training materials. Put your revenue generation strategies front and center to ensure great financial health.

For example, if you are a guest relations team member, you have great opportunities to contribute to the medical spa's success. Reserve consultations that lead to thousands of dollars; upgrade at check-in by including more treatments; make sure, at check-out, that the home care goes with them. These roles must be defined, training provided, so they're positive habits you and everyone else practice all the time.

Let's say you're an injector and have a guest coming in for Botox. You do the consultation and notice they could also use filler, but you don't make the recommendation. They get their Botox and leave. You generated around $300 in revenue, instead of $2,000-plus, simply because you didn't make a recommendation.

That recommendation would have helped the client achieve better results, but because you didn't make the recommendation, everyone involved missed out on better results—the client missed out on looking younger, and the provider missed out on earning more money.

Similar scenarios take place in medical spas and practices every day. That's why it's so important to be aware of the revenue generation process and for the team to understand its importance. It means the difference between being average and being super successful.

Here's an example of changing mindset about selling. A member named Dee is an excellent Nurse Practitioner and entrepreneur. She has a large medical spa and is working toward becoming a high achiever.

As a member, Dee has access to the S.A.C.R.E.D. system training where we teach how to implement the "Get To Know You" consultation process. During training, her spa had a phone call from a new client who wanted to come in and receive Botox, and they reserved her appointment. Dee greeted the new client when she arrived and took her into the consultation suite.

They discussed the client's goals and concerns using the intake form, and Dee recommended a customized plan worth more than $6,000 in revenue. She took a client who came in merely for Botox, and through communication and by applying the S.A.C.R.E.D. system, converted her into investing more than $6,000 to improve her image.

That's the transformation that happens when you focus on the client's needs and the sales process.

Everyone must commit to recommending solutions for everything a client needs and let them decide whether they want to do it or not.

3. **Buy-in – what's in it for the team and guests**

Here's where the rubber meets the road. The team must buy in on the sales process and the business's entire revenue generation strategy.

It all begins with the hiring process. Everyone must know the importance and value you place on your sales process. It's essential that everyone simply makes the recommendations and lets the client tell them yes or no.

Clients come to you expecting your help and recommendations, and they feel cheated if you don't tell them what's best for them. They come to you because of your expertise, reputation, and skills. If you let them leave without recommending a full treatment program and home care regimen, you cheat them out of your professional recommendations. The guest deserves to know all the available options.

What's in it for the team?

Buying in on the sales process and revenue generation strategy means you fulfill your professional obligation, improve your confidence, know you are living your purpose, and are truly helping people. You are advancing your status, expertise, and skills. Making recommendations enables you to generate more revenue and earn more money. Commit now to buy in on the importance of revenue generation.

What's in it for guests?

Guests should receive what we, in our philosophy, call a "complete guest experience." That's when you help them select treatments to be performed at the medical practice and educate them on which home care products are best for them to achieve results at home between treatments.

4. Team training to improve revenue-generating skills

Training has been my passion and purpose for my whole life. For decades, we've provided the InSPAration community with success tools that help them operate a medical aesthetic business on autopilot.

Some of our members are former football and basketball players who played for the NFL and NBA. It's always great to work with professional athletes because they truly understand the value of training. Everyone must train and perform in professional sports to stay on the team.

During one mastermind meeting, an athlete member shared with the group how often they trained and what they were required to do to stay on the team. They defined roles and strategies to win games. Every single person knew how they contributed to the team and what was expected of them. If someone didn't carry their weight or play their part, the team didn't win the game.

The same applies to business.

Fact: Billions of dollars are spent on beauty and self-care products every year. Unfortunately, most spas and medical spas aren't getting their fair share of the market. The industry is missing out on many millions of dollars that could be generated from home care recommendations and retail sales.

As a consulting firm, we receive phone calls every day from leaders who complain about their business's lack of retail sales. We ask, "Do you have a recommendation system in place with expectations, bonuses, and consequences for your team?" The answer is usually no.

If you answer no, how do you expect your team to improve its performance and achieve better results if its members are not trained and held accountable to fulfill their professional obligation—which is making recommendations?

Performance improvement must be a part of your culture and values. Training is an essential component of your business's success. It needs to be conducted often and must include role-playing.

Someone has to be responsible for training and coaching the team. Again, we return to team sports. The coach creates the game plan, and the team listens to the coach and practices what they've learned. On game day, each team member has his or her playbook down because they practiced again and again. That's role-playing.

Typically, clients tell us their team doesn't want to role-play. Many leaders give up and don't force the issue. Can you imagine a basketball or soccer player telling his coach they don't want to role-play or practice?

How long would that player stay on a winning team? You get my point.

Similarly, you and your team must role-play recommending products and treatments. The more everyone practices, the more comfortable they'll be and the more confidence they'll have recommending home care products.

Their training should include clinical knowledge, information, protocols, upgrading treatments, and how to recommend home care products. Set up a training schedule in your business and make learning a fun experience.

5. Revenue targets and performance expectations

As medical professionals, you have certain obligations to your clients and guests. Home care recommendations must be a part of the guest experience. Providing training on using products is a key principle that will help your clients, team, and business.

Set targets for home care product sales and measure your team's results regularly and often. Don't wait until the end of the month to discover that team members didn't hit their targets.

Set performance targets and expectations per day, week, and month. Measure actual sales vs. target ones. Post numbers in the team lounge, so everyone sees their numbers. Recognize those with good performance and coach others who need help.

6. Tie compensation to performance

Compensation plays a huge role in boosting revenues. Address this by tying compensation to performance. Allow team members to be paid their true worth. The more value they bring—the more products they recommend, and the more money they generate—the more they earn. Create a bonus scale based on achieving specific "revenue per guest" targets. Reward and recognize the team for making recommendations and increasing the revenue per guest. Share their success stories.

Here's your formula for calculating home care revenue per guest, which we call Volume Per Guest (VPG):

(Retail revenue) ÷ (number of guests) = (retail volume per guest)

Most people have an awakening when they calculate average revenue per guest and see how low it is and how much money they're missing out on. Decide on your targets, and pay the team based on their achievements.

7. Implement a recommendation system

It's much easier for your team to recommend home care products and treatment upgrades if you have a recommendation system in place. Systems ensure consistency, accuracy, and growth. Without a proven, effective system, your bottom line will be flat.

Fortunately, there are systems available to help you. Many medical aesthetic practice owners implement the *Don't Sell, Recommend!* with the P.R.I.D.E. system. That's the philosophy I shared earlier about delivering a complete guest experience in your facilities and at home.

The system helps your team easily identify guests' needs and concerns, then recommend appropriate home care products using the P.R.I.D.E. system. You can also develop your own system. Either way, you must have a system you can use to teach your team to improve performance and measure effectiveness.

Rewards and consequences

You must outline your expectations during employment interviews. When you're considering hiring a new employee, tell them about your business structure, culture, policies, procedures, philosophy, values, and other expectations.

Your position descriptions must outline the importance of guest satisfaction, the results employees can achieve by making home care recommendations, and your performance expectations. That must also be in your employee manual, along with rewards and consequences for when performance is not up to par.

Your potential new hire must understand these guidelines before accepting a position. Once they agree and understand your performance expectations, you can manage and implement rewards and recognition programs.

If performance is not acceptable and does not improve, consequences could progress accordingly:

- For new hires, provide additional training and coaching.
- At the first verbal warning, more training.
- At the first written warning, more training.
- At the second written warning, more training.
- If they don't improve, let them go!

The idea is to develop and train your team. Use the I.C.A.R.E. coaching model to develop your team. But if you invest in their training again and again, and they don't reach their goals, it's time for a divorce.

Focus on selecting team members who are motivated to develop their skills and grow professionally. Look for those who care about providing their guests with home care recommendations and everything they need, so you can fulfill your professional obligations.

It's time for the spa and medical spa industry to maximize opportunities and make the recommending process a habit. Set new guest experience standards for your spa, and plump up your bottom line.

Build your success library

Every business must have a success library to help train the team and lead them to success.

Training can include videos, audio, books, and manuals. They can be general, and by clinical and business departments. Having training tools helps an organization with the training process and provides a blueprint for consistency. Training can be very time-consuming and repetitive if you don't have a video training curriculum and library to teach and train from. That saves you a lot of time and money.

Members love the access we give them to the MedSpa Biz University. They don't need to spend hours creating training but can just provide the login to team members, who can then access a plethora of videos, manuals, business tools, forms, and scripts to help them improve their performance. There are programs such as Recipes for Success and much more.

Strive to do your best always, whether you've been in the industry a long time or are new. Are you doing everything you can to be the best of the best? Are your clients telling you how amazing your treatments are? If so, congratulations, you're on the right path.

If not, start training. Don't learn only at work. To be the best of the best, you must train on your own time. When you get home from work, don't watch TV. Study, practice, and rehearse. Go the extra mile, sharpen your skills, and you'll be on top of the world.

The only way to develop your skills is to seek knowledge from other successful people and experts. If you don't learn from those who are more successful than you, you won't be able to become more successful yourself. If you don't continue to learn, nothing will change.

Commit now to continue learning throughout your entire life. Read books and hire a business coach or mentor. Find someone in your company or field that can help you develop your skills. You will grow both professionally and personally.

Sports teams always have coaches that players learn from. Players don't just show up and play. Just as in sports, you must learn from a coach to perform your treatments properly and bring value to guests and the business. Be open to receiving continual help and professional coaching.

Identify each team member's responsibilities, roles, and contributions so everyone can succeed. Remember, the more you train, the better you become and the greater the results.

TAKEAWAYS

_____

_____

_____

_____

_____

_____

SHORTCUTS TO SUCCESS

- Identify and perfect your client sales journey.
- Develop your sales and recommendation process; check out the P.R.I.D.E. system.
- Train the team on your process and systems.
- Set your performance targets and goals.
- Offer rewards for great performance and clarify consequences.
- Continually train, measure, and celebrate your success.

INSPARATION MANAGEMENT BUSINESS TOOLS

- Don't Sell, Recommend! The P.R.I.D.E. recommending system
- Effective Team Building with the C.L.A.R.I.T.I. hiring system
- The I.C.A.R.E. Coaching system
- The Guest Consultation-S.A.C.R.E.D. System

CHAPTER 11

TAP INTO ONLINE REVENUE STREAMS

> *Don't miss out on additional revenue from online efforts; seize the opportunity and earn more.*
> —Dori Soukup

Many medical aesthetic business professionals only think about their brick-and-mortar business and dismiss online revenue stream opportunities. That's a big mistake. Today, your business model is not complete unless you have an online strategy to generate revenue.

In this chapter, we focus on three main online revenue streams:

1. An online shop. (Revenue from products.)

2. Online consultations. (Revenue from skincare products and treatments.)

3. Online webinars. (Revenue through education.)

Having multiple revenue sources helps protect your business against disruptions. The best way to become more essential is to generate a portion of your revenue from online strategies.

SET UP YOUR ONLINE SHOP

We always encourage clients to have online revenue streams. Some listen and do it, and some procrastinate and miss out.

When the coronavirus hit and the world shut down, the first thing we did was help all our members without an e-commerce store to launch one, so they could maintain cash flow.

It's actually very simple to include an online shop within your website. There are many e-commerce platforms to choose from, and you can be up and running in a short amount of time.

If you don't have an e-commerce site already, make it a priority to launch one. Online shopping and e-commerce continue to grow. An estimated 2.14 billion people worldwide spend more than $4.2 trillion in online purchases.

Here's some recent information from statista.com:

- 63% percent of shopping occasions begin online, and nearly half of consumers shop more on mobile than in-store.
- 51% of Americans prefer to shop online.
- E-commerce is growing 23% year-over-year, yet 46% of American small businesses do not have a website.
- 42% of online shoppers want more testimonials from e-commerce sites.
- 30% of online shoppers want more video from e-commerce sites.
- 67% of Millennials and 56% of Gen Xers prefer to shop online rather than in-store.

- 41% of Baby Boomers and 28% of Seniors will click to purchase.
- Millennials and Gen Xers spend nearly 50% more time shopping online each week (six hours) than their older counterparts (four hours).

Clearly, you need to get in the game and claim your fair share. Having a shop helps you reach a wider audience and lets you generate revenue 24/7. Yes, you can make money while you sleep.

PLAN YOUR E-COMMERCE SHOP

This list will help you start working toward launching your e-commerce site.

1. Make sure your website is responsive, mobile-friendly, and makes a great brand impression on consumers.
2. Analyze your website traffic. Set up Google Analytics to see how much traffic your site gets and make improvements to increase the count.
3. Prepare your shop's content with images and product descriptions.
4. Install Facebook Pixel code on your shop for retargeting ads and other benefits.
5. Own your site and domain name and know your login username and password.
6. Increase engagement opportunities with videos, case studies, and before and after pictures for each product.
7. Set up social media sites for your shop.
8. Select your business name and choose a legal structure.
9. Apply for an EIN number if you don't already have one.

10. Obtain an SSL certificate to stay legal and compliant.

1. **Choose your e-commerce platform**

An e-commerce platform is software that enables the commercial process of buying and selling over the internet.

When choosing a platform, make sure:

- It's user-friendly, both for you and the end-user.
- It has secure, easy payment processing. Popular payment gateways are PayPal, Authorize.net, and FirstData, among others.
- It integrates with other software.
- It's customizable.

There are many e-commerce platforms to choose from, including:

- Shopify (and Shopify Plus)
- BigCommerce
- WooCommerce
- Squarespace
- Wix

2. **Choose products to sell**

Start by identifying the types of products your target market likes. You might want to host a focus group meeting and ask some of these questions:

- What personal care products do you buy?
- What can't you live without?
- What's popular right now?
- What personal care products do you hear consumers complain about?
- Is there something you'd like to buy online but can't find?

- What are your price points?

Brainstorm some ideas and make a list of products. Here are some suggestions:

- Skincare for face, body, hands, and feet, both gifts and gift sets
- De-stress kits
- Travel kits
- Fun branded items
- Essential oils
- De-stress tools
- Hay House books, positive decks, and more
- Supplements
- Gift cards
- Gifts such as candles, robes, salts, seasonal products, and gift sets
- VIP membership enrollment capabilities

You can also attend Atlanta, New York, or California gift shows, which have unique gift ideas that clients love.

When choosing products, consider their weight, packaging, and shipping fees. Also, consider offering products that can be drop-shipped by the company providing the products.

Companies such as ZO, SkinMedica, and Colorscience let you feature their product. They'll drop-ship and give you a percentage of the sale.

Whatever products you decide on, make it an easy e-commerce shopping experience. Let your consumers shop by brand, product, concern, solution, and price. Make it effortless and memorable.

3. **E-commerce guidelines**

Create guidelines and consult an attorney to ensure your online shop policies and processes are within legal guidelines. Address the following questions:

- What are your shipping guidelines?
- Are there time limits or other restrictions to your return or cancellation policy?
- Is there a restocking charge for cancellations or returns?
- What are your refund and return policies?
- Store credit or refund? Will you fully refund charges to a credit card?
- What is your damaged products policy?
- How will you provide a secure financial experience?
- What is your privacy policy?

4. **Market your online shop**

There are many ways to drive traffic to your shop, including using your database and targeting new consumers.

1. **Use your current database.** Create a marketing campaign and email or text your clients and introduce them to your online shop. Invite them to visit and give them an offer on their first purchase. Share new products and treatments by offering specials only for e-commerce.

2. **Target new consumers.** Launch a campaign to introduce your shop to your target market. Introduce your brand, products, and treatments first. Develop trust by building relationships, and then convert those consumers into online clients and those that visit you for in-person treatments.

   Here are some suggestions to increase online shop traffic and sales:

- Write articles with keywords that help search engine optimization (SEO).
- Use QR codes with offline marketing pieces that drive traffic to your shop.
- Leave comments on blogs that link back to your shop.
- Pursue referral sites, recommendations, and reviews.
- Create branded items with your website address.
- Make YouTube videos to drive people to the shop.
- Do text message marketing.
- Use social media sites for marketing and engagement.
- Take advantage of business-to-business links.

5. **Set e-commerce goals**

If you already have a website, it's easier to add a shopping cart and plan your goals because you'll already have historical Google Analytics data to base them on. Run your Google Analytics and assess the following:

- Number of website visitors per month
- Pages visited
- Length of time on the site
- Opt-in rate
- Conversion rate from opt-in to sale
- Revenue per visitor
- Return visitors

Once you see how many visitors the site has, you can estimate the capture rate and revenue per visitor.

Recent studies indicate that **the average conversion rate for e-commerce websites is about 3 percent**.

What's a good Shopify conversion rate? **More than 4**

percent puts you in the top 20 percent of Shopify stores. More than 5.5 percent puts you in the top 10 percent.

Set your goals, measure often, and market your shop.

6. **Perform online consultations and generate revenue from skincare products and treatment sales**

When the COVID-19 pandemic began, we immediately launched the W.E.D.A.R.E. online consultation system, and it became very popular with InSPAration Management members. Clients that implemented this system continued generating revenue even though their physical businesses were closed. It was a great way to promote products and keep their clients engaged.

Some found it so beneficial that they continue doing online consultations today. A plastic surgeon member in Miami has a designated online consultation team. The team qualifies prospects and determines if they're a good fit for the particular treatment or procedure they're inquiring about.

Do you perform online consultations? If not, it's a great business opportunity to consider.

BENEFITS OF ONLINE CONSULTATIONS

Online consultations open many opportunities for you and consumers in surrounding communities, making it convenient to learn more about available treatment options and helping with the decision-making process.

An online consultation can become part of the lifetime client journey. It's a great way to begin building a relationship immediately by meeting face-to-face on Zoom or whatever online platform you use.

The process can also be used to reactivate inactive clients. The team can invite inactive clients to an online consultation visit to reconnect and inform them of the latest and greatest new treatments.

You can use consultations to prequalify opportunities and see if a consumer is an ideal client. It saves time by determining their needs and whether you can serve them or not.

A plastic surgeon client has a call center with a group of employees who perform online consultations all day. They are the number one sellers of Brazilian butt lifts, and they are extremely successful. They generate more than $1 million per month in revenue from online consultations.

SKILLS AND TOOLS NEEDED TO CONDUCT ONLINE CONSULTATIONS

You can't expect to do online consultations successfully without the tools and strategies you need to train and arm your team. Take some time to plan the entire process. Plan for success.

Some of your planning must include the following:

- A lead list (a list of clients)
- A pre-consultation discovery form for the client to complete
- A guest profile, if it's an existing client, with purchase history
- An online platform, such as Zoom or Skype
- An A-to-Z product ingredient list for reference
- Consultation and recommendation forms
- A product profile brochure, with prices by brand
- Success stories and before and after pictures
- A presentation
- Offers and payment methods

- Purchase guidelines and policies

Remember, preparation equals success.

MARKETING THE ONLINE CONSULTATION

Everything needs to be marketed, including online consultations. Most of the online consultation marketing processes can be automated. I'm not trying to create more work for you but to provide you with strategies that you plan and create once and then simply repeat on autopilot.

Your email and social media campaign to promote online consultations should include:

- An email invite, scheduling link, and confirmation, all automated
- A video invite within the email and on your website
- Social media posts that are pre-created and scheduled
- An outline of the benefits consumers will gain from the consultation
- Consumer interviews, success stories, case studies, before and after photos, and testimonials
- A website landing page where clients book an online consultation
- Enticing offers to reserve and purchase now
- A call to action, such as, "Receive a $25 gift card to apply toward any products during the consultation"

Once you kick this campaign into gear, you'll have an automated process that will help you set up online consultations and generate a new revenue stream.

When creating your marketing materials, keep this question in mind, and you'll likely increase your reservations:

"Why should I sit in front of my computer and listen to your product and treatment specialist, aesthetician, body contouring expert, weight management expert, or sexual health expert? Why should I sit in front of them?" Clarify the message.

When your message is clear and with purpose, it gives consumers reasons to reserve an online consultation. Answer the question, "Why should they reserve an online consultation?" Show what's in it for them. What will they gain, and how will you create that gain?

Use YouTube, Facebook, Instagram, and LinkedIn to get your message out and convert. When your message is out, people will know you're doing online consultations, and they'll reserve. We have seen this work over and over.

Here's what a long-time member had to say:

> *This is my fourth year as a Mastermind member. I have to say, being a member has proven to be worth the investment. Last year, Sparkle grew 72 percent over the previous year. What I love about InSPAration Management is that all their systems work. Dori is always launching new strategies to address our business needs. Highly recommend them!*
> —Madelaine Caissie, Sparkle Lifestyle & MediSpa, Moncton, Canada

Start by creating marketing materials to launch your online consultation business. Select your online consultation team and develop a motivating compensation model. Provide the team with the W.E.D.A.R.E. system training program, set a launch date, and benefit from a new revenue stream.

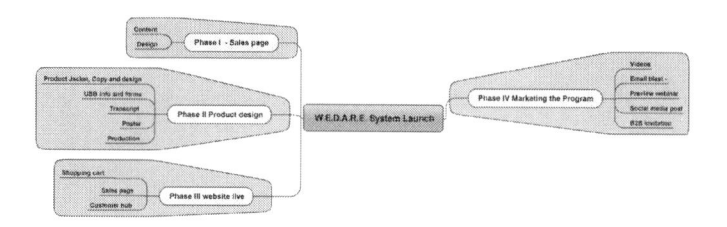

Use the Consultation Launching map, which is a complimentary download from InSPArationManagement.com/gifts

Implement the W.E.D.A.R.E. system, or another system, to launch your online business.

Here's what the W.E.D.A.R.E. acronym and system stands for:

Welcome and introduction

Engage; build rapport

Discover needs

Assess

Recommendations

Expectations

It's an online presentation structure outlined for success.

We encourage you to consider this revenue stream seriously. It's a cutting-edge strategy that most of your competitors aren't practicing. It gives you an advantage over your competition and helps you gain a larger part of the market share.

> *When you have systems in your business, your business can run on autopilot, giving you the freedom to live your life as you want to live it!*
> —Dori Soukup

You can market your business either one-to-one or one-to-many. One-to-one is like an individual consultation. One-to-many includes hosting webinars and inviting people who will benefit from learning about your topic. The one-to-many approach is a great way to get out the word to a larger audience faster and achieve great results.

You can reach people with the one-to-many method in many ways, such as:

- Speaking at conferences
- Hosting seminars
- Doing podcasts
- Writing articles, blogs, and books
- Hosting webinars

I love everything about one-to-many marketing! We've practiced these strategies for decades, and they've helped me and my team build a very successful business for all of us.

Hosting webinars is one of my favorites. It's why I have a professional filming studio in my office building. We host and film live events and shows such as *Meet the Experts* and *Dori Talks*. We also film all the business tools that we provide the industry. One-to-many is an amazing strategy that helps you connect with a large audience and grow your business very quickly.

Practicing one-to-many takes you beyond your local community, so you can spread your outreach and participate on a national or global stage. We do. We can reach a worldwide audience without even leaving the office. We love it!

Hosting webinars is a strategy we've been teaching and talking about for years, since way before they became popular during the pandemic. I'm a huge fan of the webinar.

In 2020, everyone was on Zoom trying to do webinars, but very few medical spas did them properly. A webinar's desired outcome is to educate, engage, and generate revenue—and that's where people missed the mark.

Most didn't make offers that generated revenue, so they didn't generate revenue. If you're going to apply your business efforts toward doing something, you might as well do it right, so the outcome is a win-win for everyone.

A lot of planning goes into hosting successful and profitable webinars. "Successful" means they are educational and valuable for the client and generate revenue for you.

Many clients consistently generate revenue by selling products and treatments on their webinars, generating thousands of dollars.

They accomplish their mission by providing valuable education and engaging content, making offers that promote something, and then providing a call to action to get sales. They make an offer at the end to promote what they want to sell, and attendees purchase. They host one-to-many events and apply the whole formula of success.

I'm sharing this to show you that you, too, can grow into a multimillion-dollar business by starting to apply and practice these marketing methods. I want to convince you to start marketing yourself and your company via one-to-many marketing methods so you can watch your business soar.

10 BENEFITS TO HOSTING WEBINARS AND ONE-TO-MANY EVENTS

Hosting webinars and other events that many attend benefits you in many ways. Here are just 10 positive results that will help you grow your business.

1. Staying connected, educating, and informing consumers of the latest and greatest.
2. Sharing your message and helping community members.
3. Building your reputation and positioning yourself as an expert.
4. Increasing consumer awareness of what you do.
5. Delivering valuable content.
6. Multipurpose your webinar efforts by posting them to multiple social media platforms.
7. Generating many new leads and prospects.
8. Becoming an influencer.
9. Generating revenue.
10. Expanding your reach.

Instead of making one sale in an hour, a webinar lets you reach a much larger audience, get them engaged, discuss exciting topics, make offers, and generate revenue, making many sales in that hour.

POSSIBLE WEBINAR TOPICS

What's trending right now

- The latest news on current trends
- Hot topics
- A new product of the month
- A new technique and its results
- Wellness and beauty tips
- "Ask Dr. Expert"

The possibilities are endless. Just make sure that your topics educate, provide value, and help consumers by providing solutions to their problems and concerns.

If you aren't currently offering one-to-many online marketing strategies, we encourage you to realize all the benefits this business strategy brings and start now.

Launching an online revenue stream will maximize your opportunities to generate additional revenue you otherwise wouldn't have. This opportunity is yours to seize, so take advantage of it now. And if you need help getting started, ask us.

Dare to be different!

TAKEAWAYS

_____

_____

_____

_____

_____

_____

_____

SHORTCUTS TO SUCCESS

- Develop strategies for your online revenue stream.
- Select your one-to-many strategies and begin implementing them.
- Decide who will spearhead your online revenue business.
- Practice your approach and track its effectiveness.
- Check out the W.E.D.A.R.E. system to help you strategize and implement.

INSPARATION MANAGEMENT BUSINESS TOOLS

- The W.E.D.A.R.E. system online consultation
- Success with Guest Consultations and S.A.C.R.E.D. system

CHAPTER 12

SUCCEED WITH A RECURRING REVENUE MODEL AND LOYALTY PROGRAM

> *Improve your cash flow, increase retention, and profitability, with a VIP membership model.*
> —Dori Soukup

VIP membership models and loyalty programs have been around for many years. They're used by very successful companies such as Sam's Club, Costco, AAA, churches, country clubs, health clubs, airlines, and many others. I'm sure you belong to some.

In the early 1980s, American Airlines wanted to increase retention and provide its customers with something extra special. The airline created the first frequent flyer loyalty program, which allowed travelers to accrue miles and gain benefits when they flew with American. It was one of the first companies in the country to offer a loyalty program and set the standards for the entire industry.

Even the spa industry has joined the bandwagon. Massage Envy, which offers massage memberships, opened its first location in 2002 and now has more than 1,100 locations. It's proof that the U.S. population loves to belong to clubs and be VIP members of organizations. It's why I want to encourage you to implement this model in your business.

Loyalty programs have gained popularity significantly. According to a recent study, companies spend more than $2 billion on loyalty programs every year. Statistics show the average American household belongs to about 14 different rewards programs.

If your goal is to increase your guest retention rate, it's your turn to offer a loyalty program that keeps clients coming back. Ideally, you should offer both a VIP membership model and a loyalty program to complete the lifetime client journey.

There are many benefits to offering a VIP membership model and loyalty program. First, let's identify the differences between the two.

A **membership program** is a recurring revenue opportunity where a client agrees to pay the medical aesthetic business a certain amount of money per month to receive treatments at a savings. The monthly fee is collected automatically and goes into the client's account as credit to be used on their next visit.

A **loyalty program** is when you give clients rewards for doing business with you again and again. Rewards can be gift items, points, enhancements, or something more.

As a consulting firm, we see the good, the bad, and the ugly when it comes to people setting up membership and loyalty programs.

Here are some of the most common challenges we see and how to address them:

COMMON CHALLENGES WITH MEMBERSHIP PROGRAMS

- Not charging enough or using a poor pricing model
- Not enrolling enough members
- Making the program too complicated
- Having no program management system
- Not marketing the program properly
- Offering no team training and having no presentation tools
- No one is responsible for the membership program

Instead, imagine this. You have a recurring revenue model that generates enough revenue each month to reach your breakeven point. You are collecting six figures—thousands of dollars each month—to cover your expenses and beyond. You're operating at capacity, helping many people achieve better results, seeing a better retention rate, and have financial security.

Many medical aesthetic consumers express pleasure in belonging to a community. It forces them to make time for themselves. It gives them access to expert advice regarding treatments and home care, so they can maximize their results. They enjoy the VIP savings and loyalty perks.

Having a VIP program is a win-win-win for everyone, and you must implement one to protect your business against financial disruptions.

CHALLENGES WITH LOYALTY PROGRAMS

The loyalty program mistakes we often see include a lack of planning and understating program costs. Other potential challenges:

- The reward payout is too high
- Not identifying the cost of the loyalty program within the financial budget
- Rewarding clients with treatments instead of gifts or retail products
- Too many rewards are offered at higher-than-normal payouts
- Or the opposite: the program is so lousy that no one enrolls

Before launching your rewards and loyalty programs, do the math. Be sure the numbers make sense, and your rewards are exciting and within budget.

Imagine this scenario: A client calls in and asks for a treatment, which you reserve. They come in, you do the treatment, and they leave. You pray they come back again.

I talk about this all the time. It's what I call the *a la carte business model*. It's part of how every medical spa practices.

I talked about the *autopilot model* in previous chapters. I discussed how important it is to first offer a customized treatment plan that generates thousands of dollars. Then, when it's nearing completion, you offer the VIP program and turn them into a lifetime client.

This isn't rocket science. It's a proven, effective model that leads you to generating millions!

You want your business to generate three different types of revenue:

1. **New revenue** from first visits and customized programs.

2. **A la carte revenue** from existing clients who return infrequently and pay full price.

3. **Recurring revenue** from members who return every month.

This chapter focuses on strategies that help you generate revenue from the VIP program that we help InSPAration Management members and clients implement and succeed with. It's called the C.O.P.I.E. system, and it was created with your client's best interests in mind and for your financial health.

THE CLIENT LIFETIME JOURNEY CONTINUES

Currently, consumers visit medical clinics every once in a while. Some visit more, some less, and most of the time their visits don't include a plan that's put together for them.

They end up doing some treatments here and there and buying this product and that one. They end up frustrated about spending money and not getting the results they want, and leaving. It's not a pretty scenario. It's what I call spending money on self-care instead of investing money in a personal beauty and wellness plan that works for them. That's where the philosophy of the C.O.P.I.E. system comes in.

The philosophy is that each person has a *personal image allowance* they commit to investing—a certain amount of money each year. Surveys find that consumers spend from $3,000 per year ($250 per month) to $10,000-plus per year ($800 per month) at medical spas.

The goal is to create a VIP program that entices more people to join and invest in their beauty and wellness on an annual basis, paid monthly.

That's the philosophy of the VIP membership. Members commit to an annual customized plan that helps them invest in their personal image allowance and get the best results. Other benefits include the savings they receive, the value of being a member, and the loyalty program.

8 ESSENTIAL STEPS TO LAUNCH A UNIQUE MEMBERSHIP PROGRAM

1. **Design your VIP program**

There's a lot that goes into setting up a successful VIP program. But once it's created and launched, it operates on autopilot. Your VIP program should be simple, beneficial, and provide great experiences and results.

2. **VIP member savings and your pricing model**

Most medical aesthetics offer monthly specials, but this is time-consuming, and deep discounts deplete profit lines. Your pricing model plays a key role in profitability and is best set up with two options:

- **A la carte pricing**. This is your full price.
- **VIP pricing**. This includes price reduction savings based on membership levels.

This model will help you stop discounting and depleting your profits. It's almost certainly a change in how you've been pricing treatments and products, but it's a wise shift that lets you earn your true worth and reward your most loyal clients.

Before you determine your VIP price savings, make sure you do a financial analysis to determine profit amounts after

you apply the VIP savings at each level.

3. **Membership management system**

You must have a membership management software system.

Don't attempt to launch a membership program without one. It will help you track member usage, retention, attrition, autopay, and overall program management success.

4. **Payment management**

Automated payment processing capabilities are an important management step. Be aware of failed payments and have a collection process for late payments or delinquency.

5. **Membership guidelines**

Write answers to Frequently Asked Questions (FAQs) and all the "What if?" questions, such as accrual, cancellations, multiple use, and payments. Examples of questions to address:

- Do I have to sign a contract?
- How do I pay?
- Can I let someone else use my membership?
- Can I accumulate it?
- Can I freeze my membership?
- Can I stop my membership?

6. **Market and launch your membership program**

Create your marketing materials, posters, flyers, membership cards, agreements, brochures, and update your website.

7. **VIP enrollment team training**

Achieving member enrollment success is a team effort, make sure you train your team. Setting performance expectations and rewards will help ensure your success.

ENROLLMENT PROCESS:

- Check visit habits
- Types of treatments they usually reserve
- Their profession
- How will they benefit?
- Are they ideal for the VIP program?
- Are they in the middle of a customized program?
- On average, how much money do they spend annually?

Increase member enrollments with the C.O.P.I.E. System Team Training Program.

- **C**urrent habits
- **O**ptions: A la carte vs. the VIP program
- **P**ersonal Image Fund. Spending or investing?
- **I**deal VIP program for me
- **E**nrollment and expectations

8. **Track member usage**

To ensure a long, lifetime value, make sure you track client usage. You don't want members to miss their visits and lose out financially. If they do, there's a greater likelihood they'll cancel. You want them to use their membership regularly. It's smart to send automated reminder messages to keep members engaged.

WHEN TO PRESENT YOUR VIP MEMBERSHIP PROGRAM

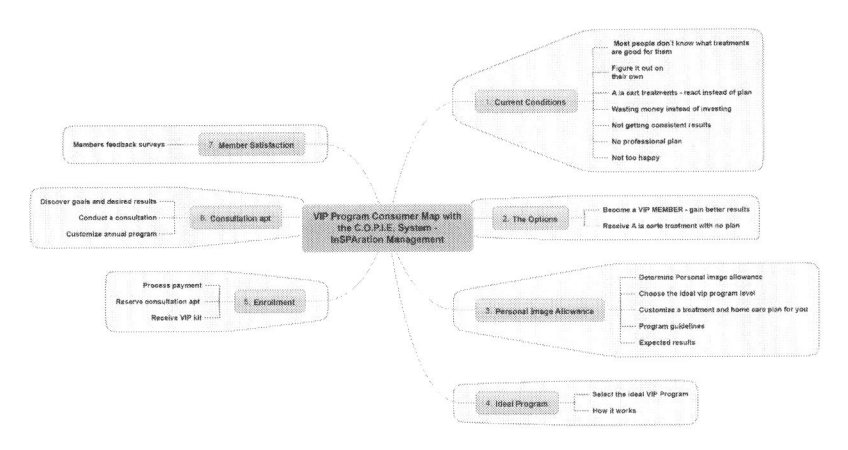

[Diagram: VIP Program Consumer Map with the C.O.P.I.E. System - InSPAration Management, showing:
1. Current Conditions — Most people don't know what treatments are good for them; Figure it out on their own; A la cart treatments - react instead of plan; Wasting money instead of investing; Not getting consistent results; No professional plan; Not too happy
2. The Options — Become a VIP MEMBER - gain better results; Receive A la carte treatment with no plan
3. Personal Image Allowance — Determine Personal image allowance; Choose the ideal vip program level; Customize a treatment and home care plan for you; Program guidelines; Expected results
4. Ideal Program — Select the ideal VIP Program; How it works
5. Enrollment — Process payment; Reserve consultation apt; Receive VIP kit
6. Consultation apt — Discover goals and desired results; Conduct a consultation; Customize annual program
7. Member Satisfaction — Members feedback surveys]

Download a complimentary VIP program map from InSPArationManagement.com/gifts.

With the business model we teach, the best time to present your VIP membership program is right after completing the final treatment of their customized program.

Note: Do NOT offer a VIP membership during a first consultation. Offering a membership right away may mean missing out on thousands of dollars you could have earned from an initial, customized program. Offer the VIP program after the client completes their customized program and achieves their desired results. The VIP program will be their maintenance to protect their investment.

INCREASE VIP PROGRAM ENROLLMENTS

Know who you're presenting to. Introducing your VIP membership without conducting proper fact-finding on the client first hinders your chances of gaining a new member.

Determine which clients are coming that day and prepare a strategy to help them.

Here are some things to know before you begin presenting or attempting to enroll clients into your VIP program.

First, observe how often the client visits your facility. Also check how long they've been receiving your services.

Next, identify the treatments they receive and how much they pay. If clients spend an average of $200 per visit, your membership price should be $250 per month. It would be a mistake to have them agree to a program that costs less. You would be losing revenue rather than gaining. Know that not everyone is right for a membership program.

Observe the client's lifestyle. What kind of work do they do? Select the membership program that would be perfect for them, based on their lifestyle.

Also, make sure the client in question is not already a member. The last thing you want to do is present a membership program to someone who already belongs. But never ask clients whether they are members or not. Everyone on the team, including Guest Relations, needs to know whether or not the client in question is a member. Do your research and your homework.

Doing the proper fact-finding before presenting shows the client you are familiar with them and their needs.

PRESENTATION TOOLS FOR VIP ENROLLMENT

Don't ask a client if they're interested in a membership. That's a close-ended question, and it results in a simple yes or no answer. Most people will say no, even if they're interested. It's human nature to say, "No thanks."

Begin explaining the membership without asking if they're interested. Be sure to give your VIP membership program a name, and don't just refer to it as a membership program.

We chose a "Flying High" theme for the InSPAration membership program to promote the idea of running your business on autopilot.

Have a brochure or flyer ready to discuss the program and highlight the positives.

Sharing a visual, such as a VIP brochure, and explaining the benefits will improve your enrollment ratio.

When presenting your VIP member program, remember to focus on the benefits. People buy benefits, not a price tag. You must know the benefits by heart and emphasize them during your presentation.

List all the program benefits in the VIP membership brochure. The brochure must also include all program options, a description of each, and how they work. It should describe the different program levels, prices, and guidelines. It's wise to include a FAQ section.

Explain the savings and value that people receive by becoming a member. The brochure needs to contain all the reasons a client should become a member: the program, its benefits, and its value and cost savings.

Go over the VIP brochure, inform them of the ideal level for them, and enroll them.

Be sure to practice your presentation until you know it by heart and are prepared to answer any questions a client may ask. Know your program, its benefits, how it works, pricing, and the enrollment process.

After presenting, my favorite closing phrase is this: "Let's go ahead and get you started. You'll love it." And, "If you decide to stop, all you need to do is give us 60 days' notice, and we can stop it for you, no strings attached. We'll take your personal image allowance and put it to great use to provide you with the results you're looking for!"

I say, "To get started, we just need to complete this form, process payment, and reserve your first treatment. I'm sure you'll love it."

If you receive any objections, you can share before and after photos to provide more proof. That also offers confidence that multiple people like them have benefited. But if you're not sold on the benefits yourself, you won't be able to convince them. Show your clients case studies and results. Do it all with enthusiasm and confidence.

Also, share information about your loyalty program, and describe all the additional benefits it offers.

MEMBER USAGE

Usage could include a client using the membership themself, giving it as a gift, or accruing it. Make sure the guest relations team keeps track of how each member uses the program. When a member doesn't take advantage of their membership, they will cancel.

VIP PROGRAM ENROLLMENT

After someone agrees to become a member, identify which program they want. Have them complete the Payment Processing Authorization form and explain the payment process.

"Julie, we want to make it super easy on you by processing your payment monthly on your credit card. You'll never have to worry about remembering to send a check or paying manually. All we need to do is complete this authorization form, and then you'll be enrolled in the VIP program. Your payment will be banked in your account, and you can use that amount each month on any treatment you wish—and the monthly savings based on your VIP level."

THE VIP PROGRAM WELCOME KIT

Have Guest Relations go over the membership welcome kit with the new member, reserve their first treatment, thank them, and say, "See you next time!"

Contents of a VIP member welcome kit:

VIP member card

- Welcome card
- Member user guide and benefits
- Tips on how to make the most of their membership
- Branded T-shirt
- Referral gift card

You must systematically implement the entire enrollment process within your practice. Everyone on the team must be capable of presenting the VIP program and enrolling new members. At your Daily Success Planning meetings, determine who will present to whom. After researching the client, the provider may present the bulk of the presentation and answer questions.

If the client chooses to become a member, Guest Relations presents the welcome kit and reserves their next treatment. If the guest relations team is busy, the provider must present the welcome kit.

If a client declines to become a member, let Guest Relations know. Guest Relations must be informed where each client stands and what was presented to them. Have open communication between providers and the guest relations team to ensure the client is not bombarded with information about the VIP program.

After a presentation, note the result in your software system and go over them in your next Daily Success Planning meeting. Periodically check the notes to see when someone was last presented with the VIP program and the results of their presentation.

VIP contract—yes or no?

A VIP membership program may be subject to attrition. Even long-time members may one day cancel their membership. It happens.

When it does happen, ask for feedback. The more feedback you receive, the more issues you can address and the more you can reduce your attrition rate.

Avoid cancellations by knowing your clients well and keeping them engaged. Show them how you can make a difference for them. The more effort you put forth, the longer they will remain members.

I'm not a fan of contracts. With today's social media, the last thing you want is for an angry client to go online and badmouth your business and practice and ruin your reputation. As long as a client gives you 60 days' notice, you can stop their membership. Just make sure they don't have a balance.

Also, not having a contract means you'll enroll more people.

Promote your VIP member program

There are all sorts of methods to promote your membership programs. You can use buttons, banners, email blasts, social media, membership cards, brochures, and testimonials. Put out a press release about your program when you first launch and promote it on all your social media and in your newsletter. These are only some of the ways to market and inform your community about your VIP program.

SUMMARY

You must ask in order to receive. Show your clients the benefits of becoming a VIP member, and they will become one. Calculate how many more clients you can see per day and week and set goals. Determine how many memberships you need to sell to reach capacity. Implement a motivating compensation for the team for when they enroll members.

Determine how you will enroll members, practice your presentation, and perform fact-finding every day. Who would be the ideal person for this program? The more presentations you give, the more comfortable you'll become with presenting.

Commit to presenting the VIP program regularly, because everyone wins when clients become members. You'll see a big difference in guest satisfaction, capacity, and revenue.

LOYALTY PROGRAM

There are several types of loyalty programs you might offer clients, but no matter which one you choose, it's important to keep it simple.

Offer clients the opportunity to join for free and earn points for every visit. You can reward them with one point for every dollar they spend. Once they reach a certain number of points, they can redeem them for gifts or products.

Select gift items that you can brand with your logo, such as robes, t-shirts, hats, and water bottles. That offers many benefits:

1. It provides your loyal clients with desirable, quality gifts.

2. Branded gifts are a great way to promote your business.

3. They show a higher perceived retail value while reducing your loyalty cost.

4. It saves money and increases retention.

The point system can also be used as a marketing tool. Do you have slow slots in your schedule? Reward your clients with double points for reserving during slow days or hours. Instead of offering promotional discounts, offer double or triple points. If your clients write reviews or "like" your Facebook page, you can offer points. Be creative.

Keep in mind that how well you manage the program is critical. If you launch a loyalty program but don't keep your clients engaged and excited about it, they won't see its value and will lose interest. That's a situation where their loyalty may go elsewhere.

TOOLS YOU NEED FOR YOUR LOYALTY PROGRAM

Make your loyalty program simple but special from the beginning. Once someone joins your loyalty program, they should receive a welcome gift containing:

- A loyalty VIP card
- A VIP t-shirt with your logo on it
- Your menu
- Your most frequently asked questions
- A referral card to pass on to others
- Product samples from your brands
- Your brochure or flyer with gifts they can claim with points

Loyalty programs are a great way to increase retention and promote your business. They also let you recognize VIP clients by providing them with special value while motivating them to keep doing business with you.

Implement both a VIP membership and a loyalty program and experience exponential growth.

TAKEAWAYS

_____

_____

_____

_____

_____

_____

_____

SHORTCUTS TO SUCCESS

- Create your VIP membership model
- Train the team how to enroll members
- Set your goals & track your efforts

InSPAration **TOOLS**

- The C.O.P.I.E. system to create your recurring revenue model and VIP membership program

MEDICAL AESTHETICS SUCCESS

Take your Business into the Black by Attending the Following Seminars

The Millionaires' Circle Seminar

Join us for the Millionaires' Circle and discover the T.M.S.P. System and chart a new path to making millions.

The Millionaires' Circle is designed to provide you with advanced business strategies that will enable you to move up to multiple seven-figure income! You will learn how to raise your prices, stop discounting and generate more revenue. The T.M.S.P. system will guide you on how to Target the affluent consumers in your community, Market to the affluent, Sell to the affluent, and Profit from the affluent. You will walk away from it with a plethora of strategies that will help you generate millions of dollars and live the life you deserve! Available virtually or in person.

Write Your Book In One Weekend

Stop competing on price, compete on expertise instead by becoming a published author.

If you are a physician, an accountant, an engineer, an attorney, or hold a professional position or own a business, the Become Published Seminar is for you. During this two-day seminar, you will learn the benefits of Authority Marketing and you will write your book in one weekend. When you become published, your expertise in your industry will be established and you will be recognized as an authority in your field. As a result, you will be able to grow your business, increase prices and enjoy more revenue and profits.

Leap Ahead Leadership Seminar

Attend the Leap Ahead seminar and gain an A-to-Z blueprint on how to operate your medical spa, wellness center, or spa successfully!

You will discover how to market your business, set financial goals, build a high-performing team, deliver a great guest experience, generate more revenue, and elevate your success! No need to reinvent the wheel, discover a proven effective business model that will result in you having more freedom, less stress, more revenue, and more profits!

Go to InSPArationManagement.com to learn more and to register!
Mention this book and receive a $500 off any event.

DORI SOUKUP

SUCCESS LIBRARY

MANUALS

VIDEOS

Shop.InSPArationManagement.com

LOOKING FOR SUCCESS?

Complimentary Success Planning Session

LET US HELP YOU CHART A SUCCESSFUL PATH!

RESERVE NOW!

Go to InSPArationManagement.com to Reserve a Success Planning Session

LIKED THIS BOOK? PLEASE LEAVE US A REVIEW ★★★★★

SCAN THE QR CODES

IN**SPA**RATION
MANAGEMENT

131 Executive Circle,
Daytona Beach, FL 32114

386-226-2550

InSPArationManagement.com